The Muslim Prayer Book

Ahmadiyya Anjuman Isha'at Islam (Lahore) U.S.A., Inc.

P.O. Box 3370, Dublin, OH 43016-0176, U.S.A.

1st Edition	:	1939
USA Edition	:	1992
Reprint	:	1994
Reprint	:	1998
New Typeset	:	2016

Library of Congress Catalog card number: 92-70900

ISBN: 978-0-913321-13-3

Ahmadiyya Anjuman Isha'at Islam (Lahore) U.S.A., Inc.

P.O. Box 3370, Dublin, OH 43016-0176, U.S.A.

Website: www.muslim.org

Email: aaiil@aol.com

614-873-1030

THE MUSLIM PRAYER BOOK

by
MAULĀNĀ MUḤAMMAD 'ALĪ

AHMADIYYA ANJUMAN ISHA'AT ISLAM — LAHORE U.S.A.
P.O. Box 3370, Dublin, OH 43016-0176, U.S.A.

TABLE OF CONTENTS

TRANSLITERATION

In this book I have adopted the most recent rules of transliteration recognized by European Orientalists, with very slight variations, as explained below, but no transliteration can exactly express the vocalic differences of two languages, and the Roman characters in which Arabic words and phrases have been spelt give the sound of the original only approximately. Besides the inability of the characters of one language to represent the exact pronunciation of the words of another, there is another difficulty in romanizing Arabic words, *viz.*, that in certain combinations the pronunciation does not follow the written characters; for example, al-Raḥmān, the sound *l* merging in that of the next letter *r*. To this category belong all the letters which are known by the name of *al-ḥurūf al-shamsiyya* (lit., *solar letters*), and they are as follows: tā, thā, dāl, dhāl, rā, zā, sīn, shīn, ṣād, dzād, ṭā, zā, lām, nūn (dentals, sibilants, and liquids). Whenever a word beginning with one of these letters has the prefix *al* (representing the article *the*), the *lām* is passed over in pronunciation and assimilated to the following consonant; in the case of all other letters, *al* is pronounced fully. This merging of one letter in another occurs also in certain other cases, for which a grammar of the Arabic language should be referred to. I have followed the written form but in transliterating the adhān (call to prayer) and prayer recital, I have followed the pronunciation, for the facility of the lay reader, writing ar-Raḥmān, and so on.

The system adopted in this work is as follows:

CONSONANTS

Arabic letters	*Sounds*	*Represented by*
ء	hamza (sounds like *h* in *hour* - a sort of catch in the voice)	'
ب	bā (same as *b*)	b
ت	tā (the Italian dental, softer than *t*)	t
ث	thā (between *th* in *thing* and *s*)	th
ج	jīm (like *g* in *gem*)	j
ح	ḥā (very sharp but smooth guttural aspirate)	ḥ
خ	khā (like *ch* in the Scotch word *loch*)	kh
د	dāl (Italian dental, softer than *d*)	d
ذ	dhāl (sounds between *z* and *th* in *that*)	dh
ر	rā (same as *r*)	r

Arabic letters	Sounds	Represented by
ز	zā (same as *z*)	z
س	sīn (same as *s*)	s
ش	shīn (same as *sh* in *she*)	sh
ص	ṣād (strongly articulated *s*, like *ss* in *hiss*)	ṣ
ض	dzād (aspirated *d*, between *d* and *z*)	dz
ط	ṭā (strongly articulated palatal *t*)	ṭ
ظ	ẓā (strongly articulated palatal *z*)	ẓ
ع	ʻain (somewhat like a strong guttural *hamza,* not a mere vowel)	ʻ
غ	ghain (guttural *g*, but soft)	gh
ف	fā (same as *f*)	f
ق	qāf (strongly articulated guttural *k*)	q
ك	kāf (same as *k*)	k
ل	lām (same as *l*)	l
م	mīm (same as *m*)	m
ن	nūn (same as *n*)	n
ه	hā (same as *h*)	h
و	wāo (same as *w*)	w
ي	yā (same as *y*)	y

VOWELS

The vowels are represented as follows:

Short vowels	ـَ	*fatḥah,* as *u* in *tub*	a
	ـِ	*kasrah,* as *i* in *pin*	i
	ـُ	*dzammah,* as *u* in *pull*	u
Long vowels	ا	long *fatḥah,* as *a* in *father*	ā
	ى	long *kasrah,* as *ee* in *deep*	ī
	و	long *dzammah,* as *oo* in *moot*	ū
	اَوْ	*fatḥah* before *wāo*	au
	اَي	*fatḥah* before *yā*	ai

Tanwīn:

ـً ـٍ ـٌ is represented by *an, in, un,* respectively. The short and long vowels at the end of a word are shown as parts of the words, as *qāla* where the final *a* stands for the *fatḥah* on *lām,* but the *tanwīn* is shown as a separate syllable, as *Muḥammad-in.*

PREFACE

A Muslim Prayer-Book has been a long-felt want. Details of the Islamic institution of prayer were first given by me in the preface to my translation of the Holy Qur'ān as long ago as 1917, and they have since been published in many booklets. The treatise I am now placing before the Muslim public, however, contains not only a detailed account of that unique institution of Islam, the five daily prayers and other congregational services such as Friday and 'Īd prayers, but also adds thereto what a Muslim ought to know regarding the most important occasions in his life, such as birth, marriage and death. To this are further added the most important prayers contained in the Holy Qur'ān and prayers for different occasions as taught in Ḥadīth.

A word of explanation may be added regarding the last mentioned prayers. Islam makes a man realise the Divine presence, not only when he is within the precincts of a house of worship but also in the midst of his worldly occupations, thus making a belief in the existence of God a real force in his life. It is for this reason that the Holy Prophet Muḥammad, may peace and the blessings of Allāh be upon him, has taught us to resort to prayer on different occasions. The underlying idea is that we should always turn to God and thus feel His presence as a reality even when engaged in our worldly pursuits.

MUḤAMMAD 'ALĪ
President
Aḥmadiyya Anjuman
Isha'at Islam
Aḥmadiyya Buildings,
Lahore: 30th May, 1938.

Nature and Value of Prayer

A belief in God is the fundamental principle of every religion; nevertheless the object of religion is not simply to preach the doctrine of the existence of God as a theory; it goes far beyond that. Religion seeks to instill the conviction that God is a living force in the life of man; and prayer is the means by which it is sought to achieve this great end. The real conviction that *God is*, comes to man, not by the belief that there is a God in the outer world, but by the realization of the Divine within himself; and this realization is attained through prayer. Though to most people, nowadays, the existence of God amounts to little more than a theory, yet in every age and among every nation there have been men who, through prayer, have realized the great truth of the Divine existence within their hearts, and have laid down their lives for the good of humanity. In their case belief in the existence of God was a moral force which not only worked an entire change in their own lives, but also enabled them to transform the lives of entire nations for centuries and change the histories of peoples and of countries. Their selflessness and truthfulness were beyond reproach, and their testimony, which is really the testimony of all nations in all ages, establishes one fact, that belief in the existence of God becomes a moral force of the first magnitude when once it is realised in the heart of man through prayer to the Divine Being; so great a moral force is it, indeed, that even the most powerful material forces give way before it. Is not the experience of those great personalities a beacon-light for others, showing them that they also can make God a moral force in their lives? The powers and faculties that are given to one man are also given to another, and through their proper use one man can do what another, before him, has done.

Again, if, apart from the experience of humanity, we consider the question rationally, prayer to God is the natural sequel of the acceptance, in theory, of the existence of God. The aspiration to rise to moral greatness is implanted in human nature more deeply than even the aspiration to rise to material greatness; but the only way in which that aspiration can be realized is to be in touch with the all-pervading Spirit, the fountain-head of purity and the source of the highest morality, and prayer is but an attempt to be in touch with Him. In the sayings of the Holy Prophet, prayer is spoken of as *munājāt* or *confidential intercourse* with the Lord. In one ḥadīth it is related that man should worship God as if he sees Him. Such descriptions of prayer show its real nature to be that of being in actual intercourse with the Divine Being.

The right development of human faculties depends upon the purification of man's inner self and the suppression of evil tendencies "He surely is successful who purifies it" (91:9). Prayer is spoken of as a means of purification for the heart "Recite that which has been revealed to thee of the Book and keep up prayer. Surely prayer keeps (one) away from indecency and evil" (29:45). Elsewhere too "And keep up prayer at the two ends of the day and in the first hours of the night. Surely good deeds take away evil deeds" (11:114). In a ḥadīth the saying of prayers is compared to washing in a river "Abū Huraira says that he heard the Holy Prophet say, If one of you has a river at his door in which he washes himself five times a day, what do you think? Would it leave any dirt on him? The Companions said, It would not leave any dirt on him (and he would be perfectly clean.) The Prophet said, This is an example of the five prayers, with which Allāh blots off all the evils of a man." There are many other ḥadīth in which it is stated that prayer is a *kaffāra*; in other words, it is a means of suppressing the evil tendencies of man. The reason is plain. In 20:14, "the remembrance of Allāh" is stated to be the object of keeping up prayer, while in 29:45, it is stated that "the remembrance of Allāh is the greatest (restraint)" upon sin. A little consideration will show that a law generally requires a sanction behind it, and behind all Divine laws which relate to the development of man and to his moral betterment, the only sanction is a belief in the great Author of those laws. The oftener, therefore, a man reverts to prayer, to that state in which disengaging himself from all worldly attractions, he feels the Divine presence as an actual fact, the greater is his certainty about the existence of God, and the greater the restraint upon the tendency to break that law. Prayer, thus, by checking the evil tendencies of man, purifies his heart of all evil, and sets him on the right road to the development of his inner faculties.

The Five Daily Prayers

I. Regulation of Prayer

For a Muslim his prayer is his spiritual diet, of which he partakes five times a day. Those who think that it is too often should remember how many times daily they require food for their bodies. Is not spiritual development much more essential than physical development? Is not the soul more valuable than the body? If food is needed several times daily to minister to the needs of the body, is not spiritual refreshment at the same time badly needed? Or, if the body would be starved if it were fed only on the seventh day, has not the soul been actually starved by denying to it even the little which it could get after six days? The founder of Christianity himself emphasized this when he said "Man shall not live by bread alone, but by every word that proceedeth out of the mouth of God" (Matt. 4:4). What Christ taught in words has been reduced to a practical form by the Holy Prophet Muhammad.

It may be noted that while other religions have generally set apart a whole day for Divine service, on which other work is not to be done, Islām has given quite a new meaning to Divine service by introducing prayer into the everyday affairs of men. A day is not here set apart for prayer, and in this sense no sabbath is known to Islām. Islām requires that a Muslim should be able to disengage himself from all worldly occupations and resort to his prayers, even when he is most busy. Hence it is also that Islām has done away with all institutions of monkery, which require a man to give up all worldly occupations for the whole of his life in order to hold communion with God. It teaches that communion with God may be held even when man is most busy with his worldly occupations, thus making possible that which was generally considered impossible before its advent.

But while Islām has given permanence to the institution of prayer by requiring its observance at stated times and in a particular manner, it has also left ample scope for the individual himself to select what portions of the Holy Qur'ān he likes and to make what supplications his soul yearns after. General directions have no doubt been given, and on these the whole of the Muslim world is agreed, for these directions were necessary to secure regularity, method, and uniformity, but in addition to these, ample scope has been left for the individual to give vent to his own feelings before the great Maker of the universe. As regards the time and mode of prayer, the following directions will be sufficient for the information of the ordinary reader.

II. Times of Prayer

The saying of prayer is obligatory upon every Muslim, male or female, who has attained to the age of discretion. It is said five times a day as follows:—

1. *Ṣalāt al-Fajr*, or the morning prayer, is said after dawn and before sunrise.

2. *Ṣalāt al-Ẓuhr*, or the early afternoon prayer, is said when the sun begins to decline, and its time extends till the next prayer. On Fridays, the Friday service takes the place of this prayer.

3. *Ṣalat al-'Aṣr*, or the late afternoon prayer, is said when the sun is about midway on its course to setting, and its time extends to a little before it actually sets.

4. *Ṣalāt al-Maghrib*, or the sunset prayer, is said immediately after the sun sets.

5. *Ṣalāt al-'Ishā*, or the early night prayer, is said when the red glow in the west disappears, and its time extends to midnight. But it must be said before going to bed.

When a person is sick or on a journey, or when there is rain, the early afternoon and the late afternoon prayers may be said in conjunction, and so also the sunset and early night prayers.

Besides these five obligatory prayers there are two optional ones. The first of these is the *Ṣalāt al-Lail*, the *taḥajjud*, or the late night prayer, which is said after midnight, after being refreshed with sleep, and before dawn. This prayer is specially recommended in the Holy Qur'ān. The other is known as the

Ṣalāt al-D͟zuḥā, and it may be said at about breakfast time. This is the time at which the two ʻĪd prayers are said.

III. *Wud͟zū* or Ablution

Before saying prayers it is necessary to wash those parts of the body which are generally exposed. This is called *wud͟zū*, or ablution. This ablution is performed thus:—

1. The hands are cleansed, washing them up to the wrists.
2. Then the mouth is cleansed by means of a toothbrush or simply with water.
3. Then the nose is cleansed within the nostrils with water.
4. Then the face is washed.
5. Then the right arm, and after that the left arm, is washed up to the elbow.
6. The head is then wiped over with wet hands, the three fingers between the little finger and the thumb of both hands being joined together.
7. The feet are then washed up to the ankles, first the right foot and then the left.

But if there are socks on, and they have been put on after performing an ablution, it is not necessary to take them off; the wet hands may be passed over them. They should be taken off, however, and the feet washed once in every twenty-four hours. The same practice may be resorted to in case the boots are on, but it would be more decent to take off boots when going into a mosque.

A fresh ablution is necessary only when a man has answered a call of nature or has been asleep.

In cases of intercourse between husband and wife, *g͟husl* or washing of the whole body is necessary.

When a person is sick, or when access cannot be had to water, what is called *tayammum* is performed in place of *wud͟zū* or *g͟husl*. *Tayammum* is performed by touching pure earth with both hands and then wiping over with them the face and the backs of the hands.

IV. The *Adhān*

The *adhān* (call to prayer) is called out at the prayer time, five times daily. It consists of the following sentences, uttered in the order given in a loud voice by the crier standing with his face to the *qibla*[1]- with both hands raised to his ears:—

Allāhu Akbar, Allāhu Akbar, Allāhu Akbar, Allāhu Akbar.

اَللّٰهُ اَكْبَرُ اَللّٰهُ اَكْبَرُ
اَللّٰهُ اَكْبَرُ اَللّٰهُ اَكْبَرُ

"Allāh is the Greatest" (repeated four times).

Ashhadu al lā ilāha illa-llāh, Ashhadu al lā ilāha illa-llāh.

اَشْهَدُ اَنْ لَّآ اِلٰهَ اِلَّا اللّٰهُ
اَشْهَدُ اَنْ لَّآ اِلٰهَ اِلَّا اللّٰهُ

"I bear witness that nothing deserves to be worshipped except Allāh (repeated twice).

Ashhadu anna Muḥammadar Rasūlu-llāh, Ashhadu anna Muḥammadar Rasūlu-llāh.

اَشْهَدُ اَنَّ مُحَمَّدًا رَّسُوْلُ اللّٰهِ
اَشْهَدُ اَنَّ مُحَمَّدًا رَّسُوْلُ اللّٰهِ

"I bear witness that Muḥammad is the Messenger of Allāh" (repeated twice).

Ḥayya 'ala ṣ ṣalā, Ḥayya 'ala-ṣ-ṣalā.

حَيَّ عَلَى الصَّلٰوةِ
حَيَّ عَلَى الصَّلٰوةِ

"Come to prayer" (repeated twice, turning the face to the right).

Ḥayya 'ala-l-falāḥ, Ḥayya 'ala-l-falāḥ.

حَيَّ عَلَى الْفَلَاحِ
حَيَّ عَلَى الْفَلَاحِ

"Come to success" (repeated twice, turning the face to the left).

Allāhu Akbar, Allāhu Akbar.

اَللّٰهُ اَكْبَرُ اَللّٰهُ اَكْبَرُ

---

1. *Qibla* means *the direction towards which one turns his face*. The Muslims are required to turn their faces towards Ka'bah, the sacred House at Makkah, when saying their prayers. All mosques are built so as to face the Ka'bah.

"Allāh is the Greatest" (repeated twice).

Lā illāha illa-llāh.

لَآ اِلٰهَ اِلَّا اللّٰهُ

"Nothing deserves to be worshipped except Allāh".

The following sentence is added in the call to the morning prayer after *ḥayya 'ala-l-falāḥ*:

Aṣ-ṣalātu khairum-min-an-naum,
Aṣ-ṣalātu khairum-min-an-naum,

اَلصَّلٰوةُ خَيْرٌ مِّنَ النَّوْمِ

اَلصَّلٰوةُ خَيْرٌ مِّنَ النَّوْمِ

"Prayer is better than sleep" (repeated twice).

When the call to prayer is finished, the crier as well as the hearers make a petition in the following words:—

Allāhu-mma Rabba hādhihi-d-da 'wati-t-tāmmati wa-ṣ- ṣalāti-l-qā'imati āti Muḥammada-ni-l wasīlata wa-l-fadzīlata waddarajata-rrafī'ata wa-b'athhu maqāmam maḥmudan-illadhi wa'adta-hū.

اَللّٰهُمَّ رَبَّ هٰذِهِ الدَّعْوَةِ التَّآمَّةِ
وَالصَّلٰوةِ الْقَآئِمَةِ اٰتِ مُحَمَّدَا
نِ الْوَسِيْلَةَ وَالْفَضِيْلَةَ وَالدَّرَجَةَ
الرَّفِيْعَةَ وَابْعَثْهُ مَقَامًا مَّحْمُوْدَا
نِ الَّذِيْ وَعَدْتَّهُ

"O Allāh! Lord of this perfect call and ever-living prayer, grant to Muḥammad nearness and excellence and raise him to the position of glory which Thou hast promised him."

V. The Service

The service consists ordinarily of two parts, one part, called the *fardz*,[2] to be said in congregation, preferably in a mosque, with an Imām leading the service; the second part, called *sunna*,[3] to be said alone. But when a man is unable to say his

2. *Fardz*, means literally *what is obligatory*.
3. *Sunna* means *the Prophet's practice*.

prayer in congregation, the *fardz* may be said like the *sunna*, alone.

Each part consists of a certain number of *rak'as* as explained further on.

The *Fajr*, or morning prayer, consists of two *rak'as* (*sunna)* said alone, followed by two *rak'as (fardz)* said in congregation.

The *Ẓuhr*, or early afternoon prayer, is a longer service consisting of four *rak'as (sunna)* said alone followed by four *rak'as (fardz)* said in congregation and followed again by two *rak'as (sunna)* said alone.

In the Friday service held at the time of *Ẓuhr*, which takes the place of the sabbath of some other religions, the four *rak'as (sunna*) said alone and the four *rak'as (fardz)* said in congregation are reduced each to two, but the *fardz* are preceded by a sermon *(khuṭba)*.

The *'Aṣr*, or the late afternoon prayer, consists of four *rak'as (fardz)* said in congregation.

The *Maghrib*, or the sunset prayer, consists of three *rak'as (fardz)* said in congregation, followed by two *rak'as (sunna)* said alone.

The *'Ishā*, or early night prayer, consists of four *rak'as (fardz)* said in congregation followed by two *rak'as (sunna)*, said alone, again followed by three *rak'as (witr)* said alone.

The *Taḥajjud*, or late night prayer, consists of eight *rak'as (sunna)* said in twos.

The *Dzuḥā*, or the before-noon prayer, may consist of two or four *rak'as*.

The *'Īd* prayer consists of two *rak'as (sunna)* said in congregation, being followed by a sermon or *khuṭba*.

When a person is journeying, the *sunna* are dropped in every one of the prayers except the morning prayer, and the four *rak'as (fardz)* in each of the *Ẓuhr*, the *'Aṣr* and the *'Ishā* prayers are reduced to two. When one is aware that his stay at a particular place in his journey will be ten days or more, the complete service should be performed (opinions differ on the length of stay at a particular place).

VI. Congregational Service

When there are two or more persons, they should form a *jamā'a*, congregation[4], one of them acting as the *Imām*, or the leader; but when a person is alone, he may say the *fardz* alone, as he does the *sunna*.

Two chief features of the Muslim congregational service are that the service may be led by anyone, the only condition being that he should know the Qur'ān better than the others, and that he should excel the others in righteousness and in the performance of his duties towards God and His creatures. The second is that not the least distinction of caste or rank or wealth is to be met with in a Muslim congregation: even the king stands shoulder to shoulder with the least of his subjects.

To announce that the congregational prayer is ready, the *iqāma* **(Illustration A)** is pronounced in a loud voice, though not so loud as the *adhān*. The sentences of the *adhān* are also the sentences which form the *iqāma*, but with two differences. Those in the *adhān* are with the exception of the concluding *lā*

4. The whole Muslim body that can assemble in one place, both men and women, must gather at the appointed time, praise and glorify God, and address their petitions to Him in a body. All people stand shoulder to shoulder in a row, or in several rows, as the case may be, their feet being in one line, and one person, chosen from among them and called the *Imām*, which means *leader*, leads the prayer and stands in front of all. If, however, there are women in the congregation, they form a row by themselves at the back, and after the congregational prayer is over the men are not allowed to leave their places until the women have gone out. The distance between the Imām and the first row, or between the different rows, is such that the persons in each row may be able to prostrate themselves, so that their heads may be almost at the feet of the front row. This distance would generally be four feet. The smallest number of people that can form a congregation is two, one leading the prayer and the other following, and these two stand together, the Imām a little ahead, say about six inches, and standing to the left while the follower stands on the right. If a third person joins while the prayer is thus being led, either the Imām moves forward or the person following moves backward, so that the two who follow form a row. The people who stand behind are called *muqtadūn* or *followers*, and the discipline is so perfect that the followers are bound to obey the Imām, even though he may make a mistake, though they have the right to point out the mistake, by pronouncing the words *subḥan-Allāh* (glory be to Allāh). This amounts to a hint that God alone is free from all defects, such being the meaning of the word *subḥāna*. It is however the judgment of the Imām which is the decisive factor, and the followers, after giving the hint, must still obey him.

ilāha ill-allāh repeated twice, the starting *Allāhu Akbar* alone being pronounced four times; but in the *iqāma* all these sentences may be uttered only once. The second difference is that after *ḥayya 'ala l-falāḥ*, the following sentence is uttered twice:

Qad qāmati-ṣ-ṣalā. قَدْ قَامَتِ الصَّلٰوةُ

"Prayer is ready."

The additional words of the morning *adhān* do not find a place in the *iqāma*.

As regards the service itself, the Imām reads aloud the *Fātiḥa* and the portion of the Holy Qur'ān that follows the *Fātiḥa*, in the morning prayer and the first two *rak'as* of the sunset and early night prayers, while in the remaining *rak'as* and in all other prayers, these are repeated in a low voice audible only to the reciter; the *takbirs* and all other *dhikr* announcing the change of position are, however, uttered in a loud voice in all congregational prayers.

VII. What Constitutes One *Rak'a*

As already remarked, each prayer consists of several *rak'as* of *fardz*, or *fardz* and *sunna*. One *rak'a* is completed as follows:

1. Both hands are raised up to the ears in a standing position with the face towards the *qibla*, while the words *Allāhu Akbar* (Allāh is the Greatest of all) are uttered, and this is called the *takbir taḥrima*. **(Illustration B).**

2. Then comes *qiyām*. **(Illustration C).** The right hand is placed upon the left over the breast or a little lower while the standing position is maintained, and the following prayer called *istiftāḥ* is that which is generally adopted:

Ṣubḥāna-ka-llāhu-mma wa bi-ḥamdi-ka wa tabāraka-smu-ka wa ta'ālā jaddu-ka wa lā ilāha ghairu-ka.

سُبْحَانَكَ اللّٰهُمَّ وَبِحَمْدِكَ وَ
تَبَارَكَ اسْمُكَ وَتَعَالٰى جَدُّكَ
وَلَآ اِلٰهَ غَيْرُكَ

"Glory to Thee, O Allāh, and Thine is the praise, and blessed is Thy name, and exalted is Thy majesty, and there is none to be served besides Thee."

The following is a longer prayer:

Īnnī wajjahtu wajhiya li-lladhi faṭara-s-samāwāti wa-l-ardza ḥanīfan wa mā ana mina-l-mushrikīn. Inna ṣalātī wa nusukī wa maḥyāya wa mamātī li-Lāhi Rabbi-l-'ālamīn; lā sharīka la-hū wa bi-dhālika umirtu wa ana mina-l-Muslim-in. Allāhu-mma anta-l-Maliku lā ilāha illā anta, anta Rabbī wa ana 'abdu-ka, ẓalamtu nafsī wa-'taraftu bi-dhanbī fa-ghfir-lī dhunūbī jami'-an lā yaghfiru-dh-dhunūba illā anta; wa-hdi-nī li-aḥsani-l-akhlāqi lā yahdi li-aḥsani hā-illā anta wa-ṣrif 'anni sayyi'a-hā lā yaṣrifu sayyi'ahā illā anta.

إِنِّي وَجَّهْتُ وَجْهِيَ لِلَّذِي فَطَرَ
السَّمٰوٰتِ وَالْأَرْضَ حَنِيفًا وَمَا أَنَا
مِنَ الْمُشْرِكِينَ ○ إِنَّ صَلَاتِي وَنُسُكِي
وَمَحْيَايَ وَمَمَاتِي لِلّٰهِ رَبِّ الْعٰلَمِينَ ○
لَا شَرِيكَ لَهُ وَبِذٰلِكَ أُمِرْتُ وَأَنَا
مِنَ الْمُسْلِمِينَ ○ اللّٰهُمَّ أَنْتَ الْمَلِكُ
لَا إِلٰهَ إِلَّا أَنْتَ أَنْتَ رَبِّي وَأَنَا
عَبْدُكَ ظَلَمْتُ نَفْسِي وَاعْتَرَفْتُ
بِذَنْبِي فَاغْفِرْ لِي ذُنُوبِي جَمِيعًا لَا
يَغْفِرُ الذُّنُوبَ إِلَّا أَنْتَ وَاهْدِنِي
لِأَحْسَنِ الْأَخْلَاقِ لَا يَهْدِي
لِأَحْسَنِهَا إِلَّا أَنْتَ وَاصْرِفْ عَنِّي
سَيِّئَهَا لَا يَصْرِفُ سَيِّئَهَا إِلَّا أَنْتَ

Illustration A

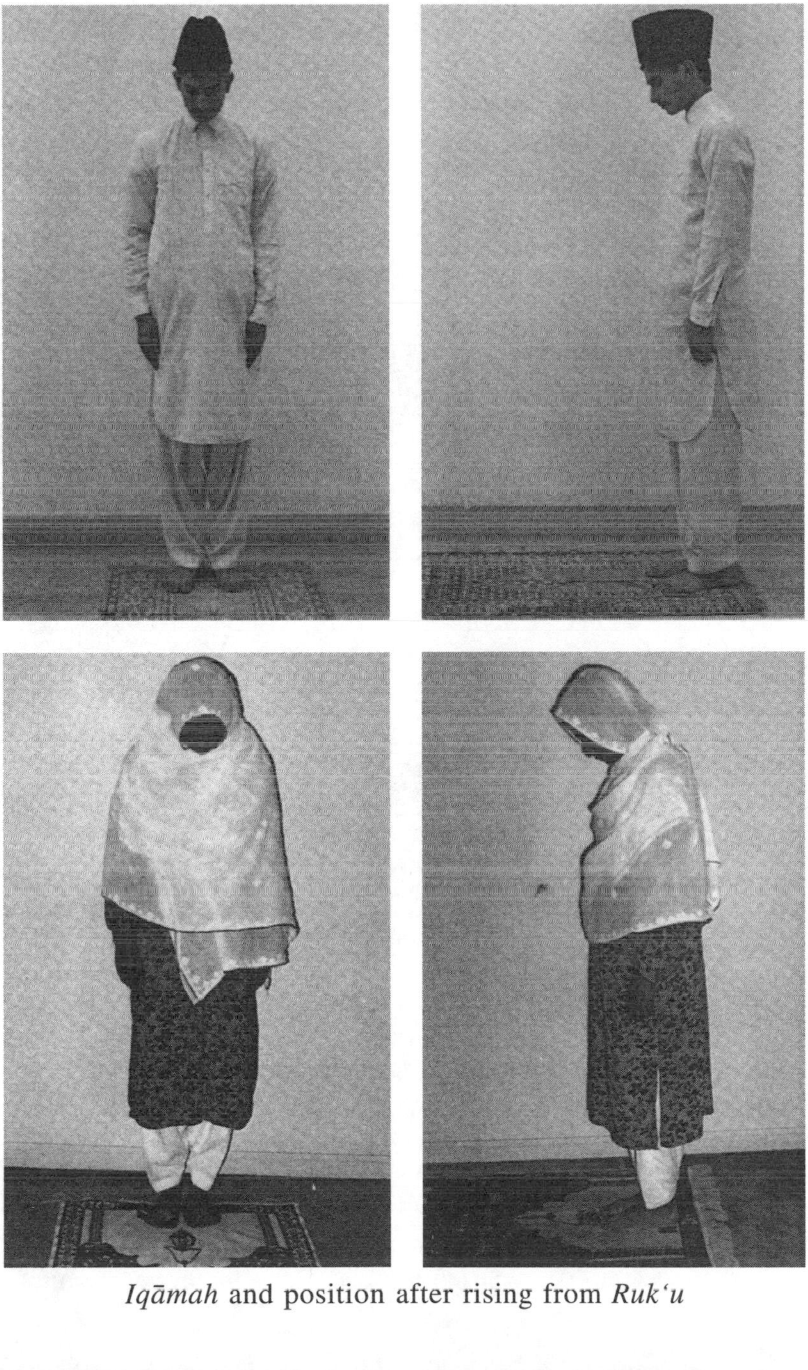

Iqāmah and position after rising from *Ruk'u*

Illustration B

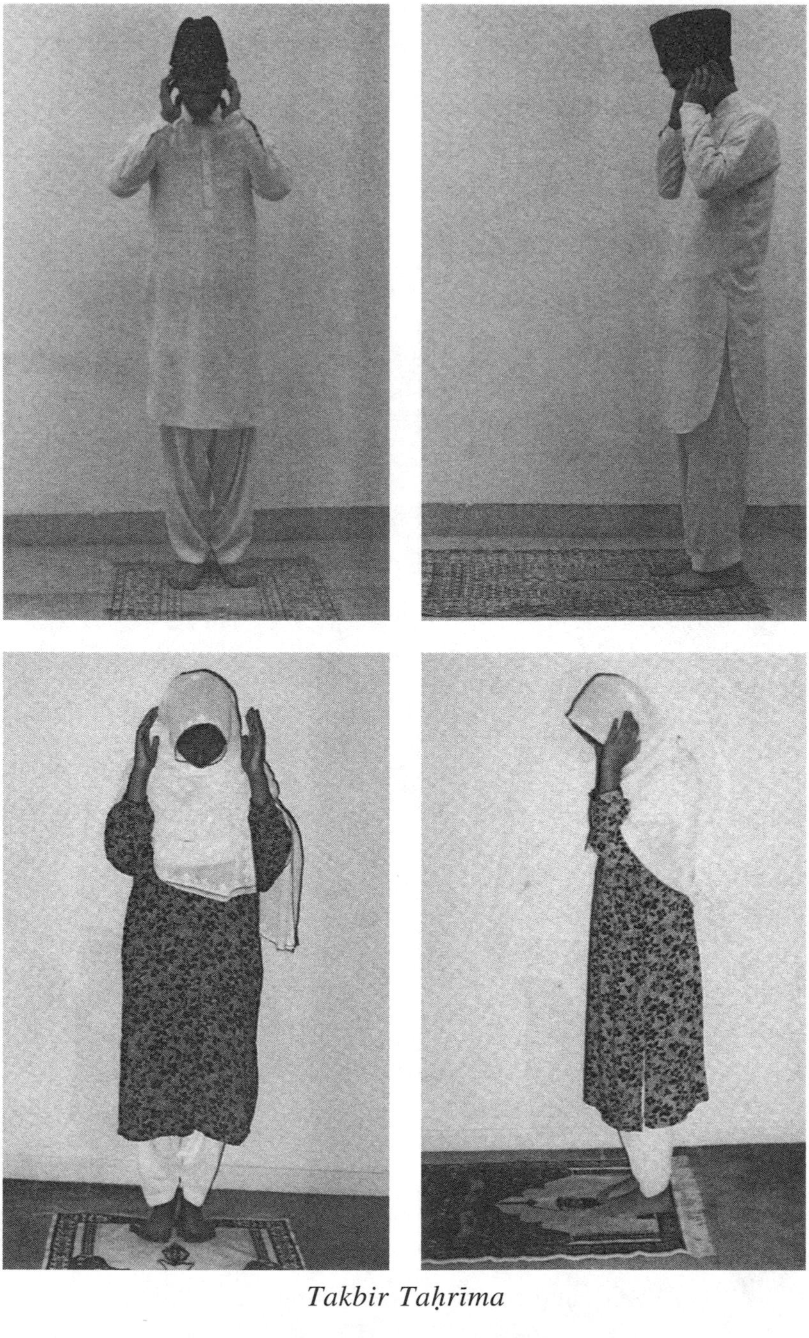

Takbir Taḥrīma

Illustration C

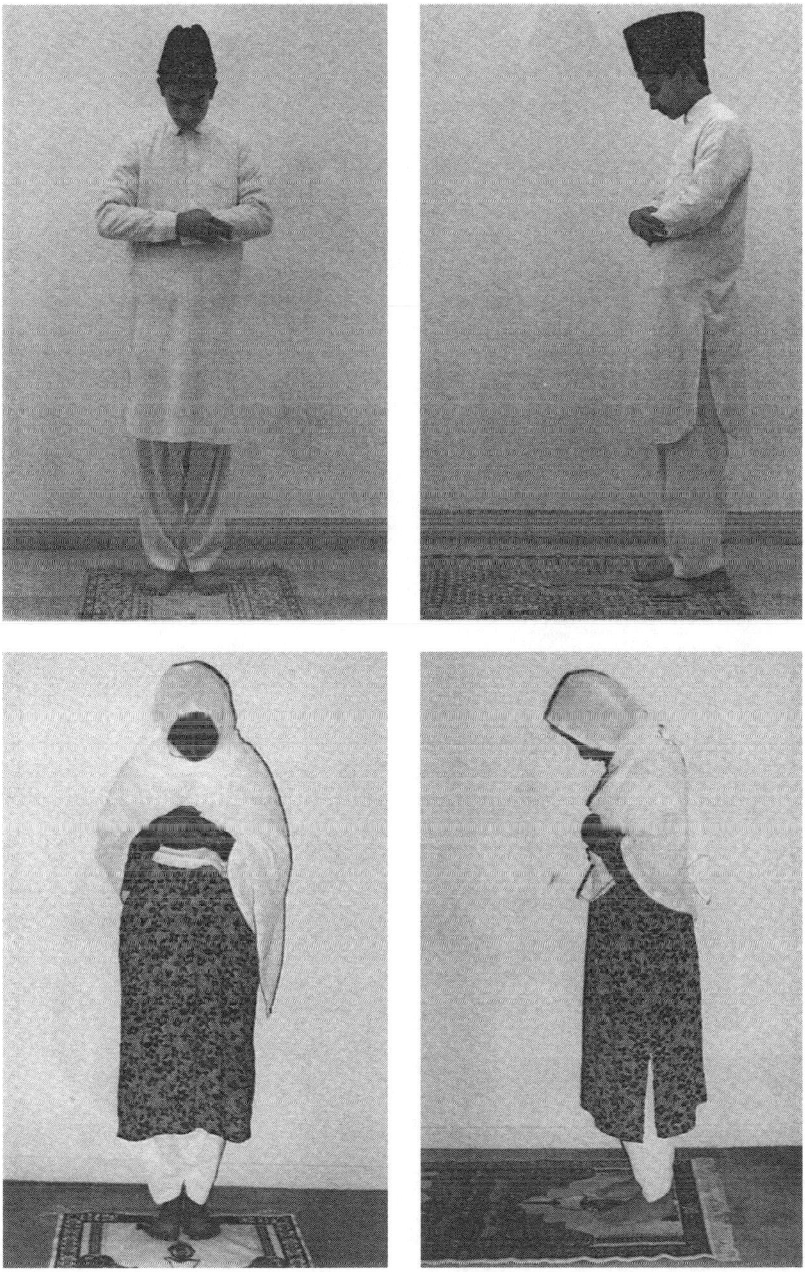

Qiyām

Illustration D

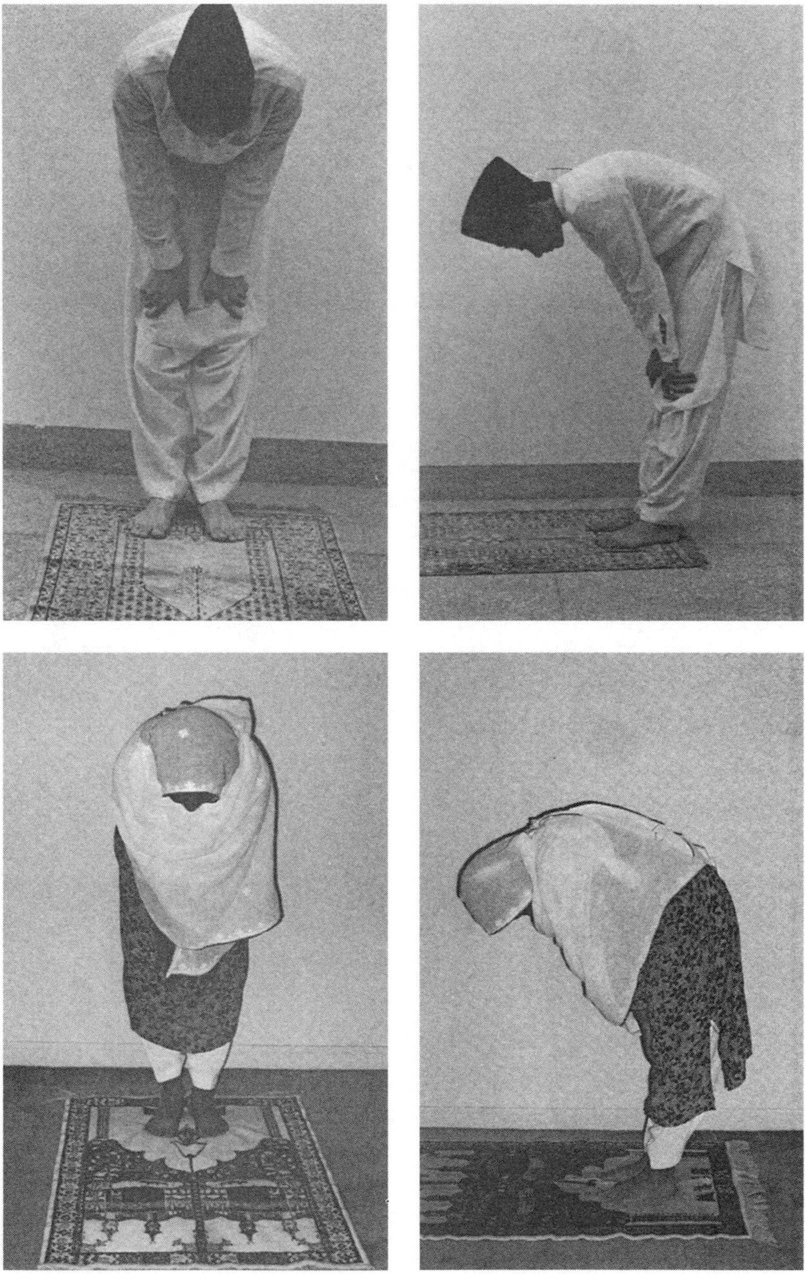

Ruk'u

Illustration E

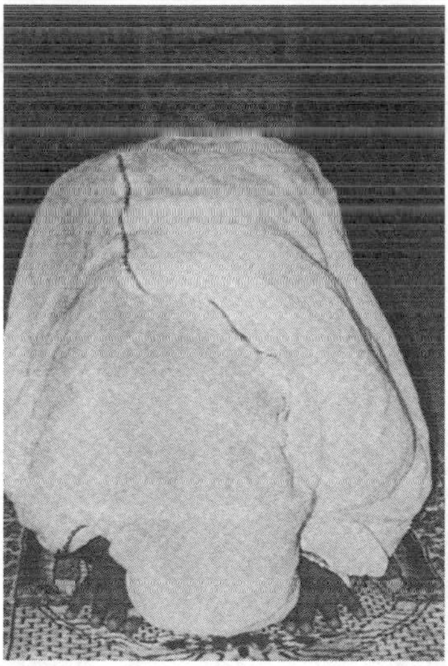

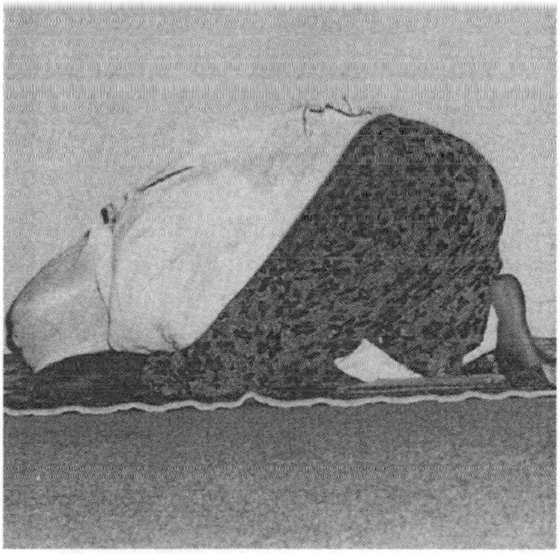

Sajdah

Illustration F

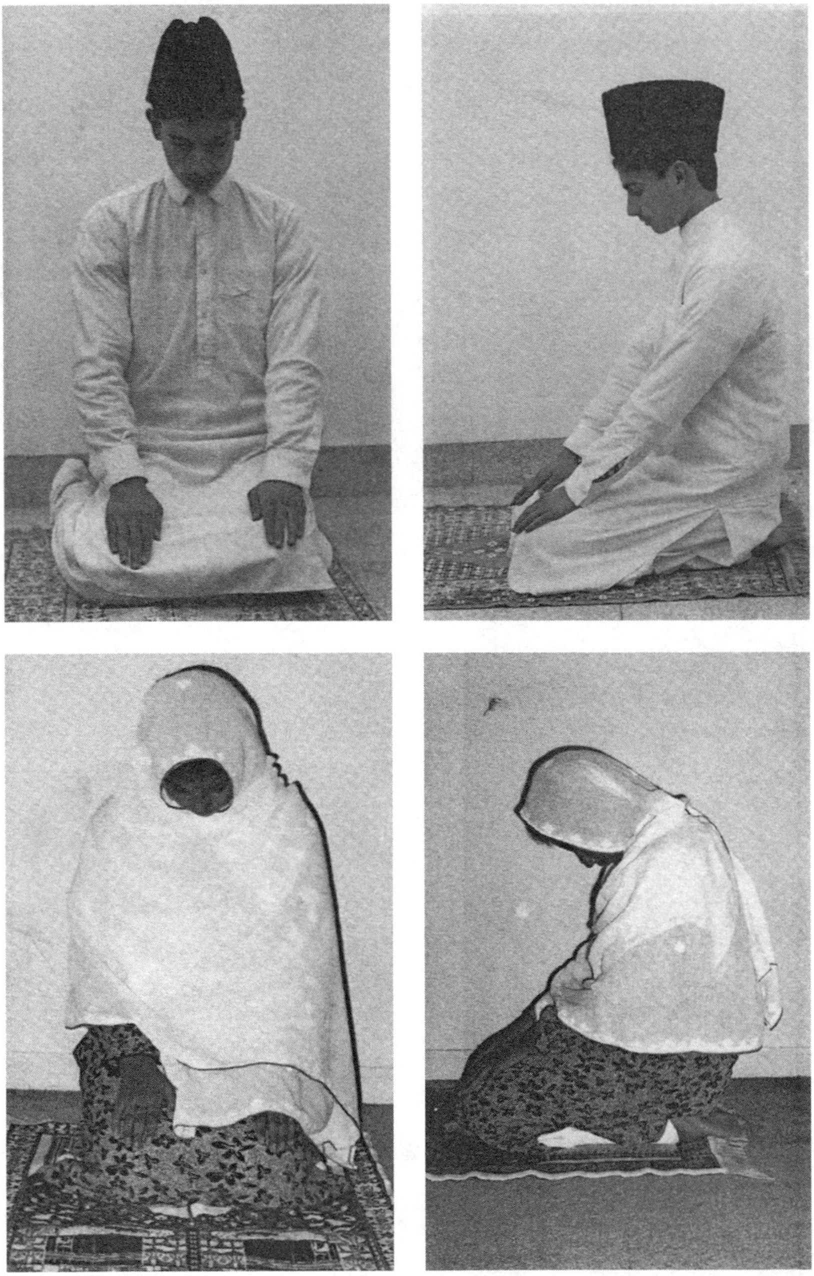

Jalsa and *Qa'da*

Illustration G

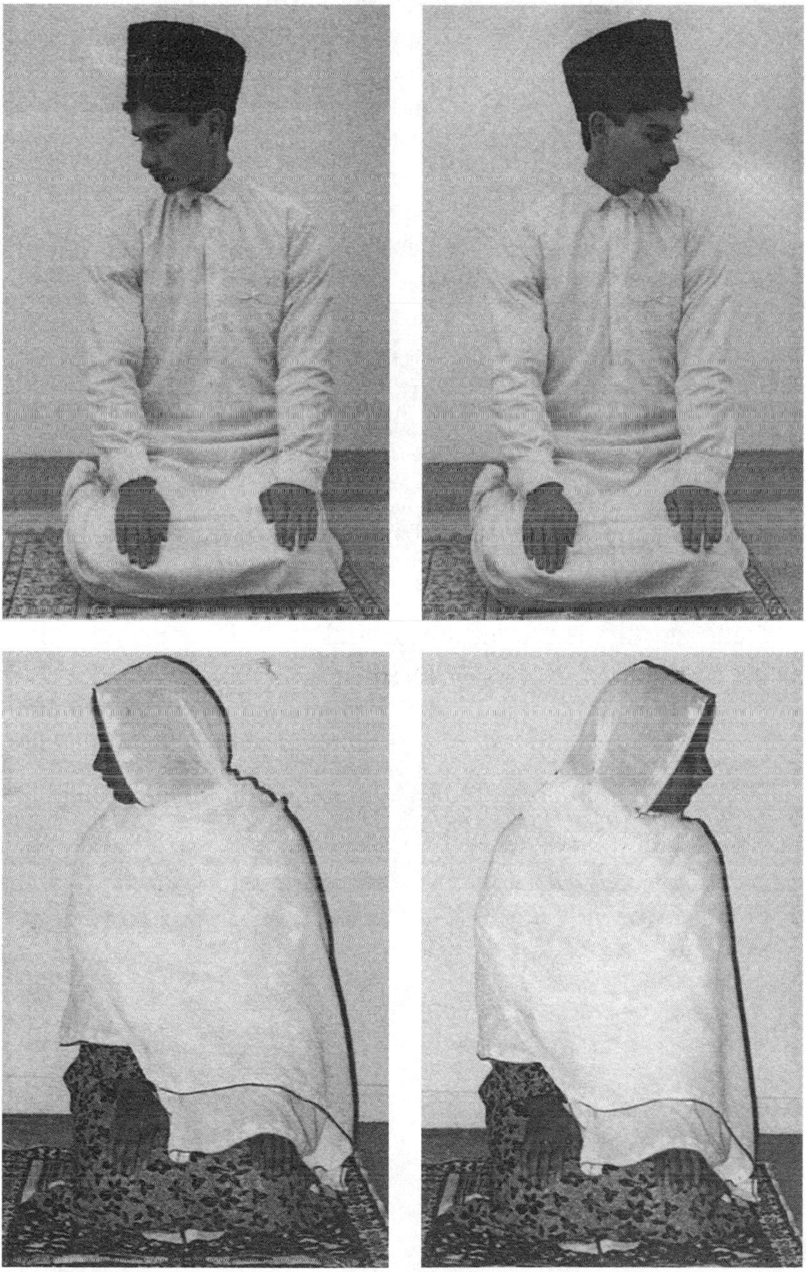

Taslīm

"Surely I have turned myself, being upright wholly to Him Who originated the heavens and the earth and I am not of the polytheists. Surely my prayer and my sacrifice and my life and my death are for Allāh, the Lord of the worlds, no associate has He; and this I am commanded and I am one of those who submit. O Allāh! Thou art the King, none is to be served but Thee; Thou art my Lord and I am Thy servant; I have been unjust to myself and I confess my shortcomings so forgive Thou all my shortcomings, for none forgives the shortcomings but Thou. O Allāh! guide me to the best of morals, none guides to the best of them but Thou, and turn away from me bad morals, none can turn away bad morals but Thou."

Either of the above prayers is followed by the word:

A'ūdhu bi - llāhi minash-shaiṭāni-r-rajīm.	أَعُوْذُ بِاللّٰهِ مِنَ الشَّيْطٰنِ الرَّجِيْمِ

"I seek the refuge of Allāh from the accursed devil."

After this the *Fātiḥa*, the first chapter of the Holy Qur'ān, is recited, and this is the most essential part of the prayer, being repeated in every *rak'a*. It runs thus:

Bi-smi-llāhi-r-Raḥmāni-r-Raḥim.	بِسْمِ اللّٰهِ الرَّحْمٰنِ الرَّحِيْمِ ۝
1. *Al-ḥamdu li-llāhi Rabbi-l-'alamīn.*	اَلْحَمْدُ لِلّٰهِ رَبِّ الْعٰلَمِيْنَ ۝
2. *Ar-Raḥmāni-r-Raḥīm.*	الرَّحْمٰنِ الرَّحِيْمِ ۝
3. *Māliki yaumi-d-dīn.*	مٰلِكِ يَوْمِ الدِّيْنِ ؕ
4. *Iyyā-ka na'budu wa iyyā-ka nasta'īn.*	اِيَّاكَ نَعْبُدُ وَاِيَّاكَ نَسْتَعِيْنُ ؕ
5. *Ihdi-na-ṣ-ṣirāṭa-l-mu-staqīm.*	اِهْدِنَا الصِّرَاطَ الْمُسْتَقِيْمَ ۝
6. *Ṣirāṭa - lladhīna an'amta 'alaihim.*	صِرَاطَ الَّذِيْنَ اَنْعَمْتَ عَلَيْهِمْ ۝
7. *Ghairi-l-magh dzūbi 'alai-him wala-dz-dzāllīn.*	غَيْرِ الْمَغْضُوْبِ عَلَيْهِمْ وَلَا الضَّآلِّيْنَ ۝

"In the name of Allāh, the Beneficent, the Merciful.

1. All praise is due to Allāh, the Lord of the worlds.
2. The Beneficent, the Merciful.
3. Master of the Day of Requital.
4. Thee do we serve and Thee do we beseech for help.
5. Guide us on the right path.
6. The path of those on whom Thou hast bestowed favours.
7. Not those upon whom wrath is brought down, nor those who go astray."

At the close of the above is said *Āmīn – i.e., Be it so.* Then any portion of the Qur'ān which the worshipper has memorized is recited. Generally one of the shorter chapters at the close of the Holy Book is recited,[5] and the chapter termed *al-Ikhlāṣ* is the one recommended for those who are unacquainted with the Qur'ān. This is as follows:

Bi-smi-llāhi-r-Raḥmāni-r-Raḥīm.
1. *Qul huwa-llāhu Aḥad.*
2. *Allāhu-ṣ-Ṣamad.*
3. *Lam yalid wa lam yūlad.*
4. *Wa lam yaku-llahu kufuwan aḥad.*

بِسْمِ اللّٰهِ الرَّحْمٰنِ الرَّحِيْمِ
قُلْ هُوَ اللّٰهُ اَحَدٌ
اَللّٰهُ الصَّمَدُ
لَمْ يَلِدْ وَلَمْ يُوْلَدْ
وَلَمْ يَكُنْ لَّهٗ كُفُوًا اَحَدٌ

"In the name of Allāh, the Beneficent, the Merciful.

1. Say, He, Allāh, is One.
2. Allāh is He on Whom all depend.
3. He begets not nor is He begotten.
4. And none is like Him."

3. Then saying *Allāhu Akbar*, the worshipper lowers his head down, so that the palms of the hands reach the knees. In this position, which is called *Rukū'* **(Illustration D)** the following words expressive of Divine glory and majesty are repeated at least three times:

5. The Qur'anic prayers quoted further on may serve the same purpose.

Subḥāna Rabbiya-l-'Aẓīm

سُبْحَانَ رَبِّيَ الْعَظِيْمِ

"Glory to my Lord the Great."

4. After this, the standing position is assumed with both arms at the sides **(Illustration A)**, with the words:

Sami'a-llāhu-li-man ḥamidah
Rabba-nā la-ka-l-ḥamd.

سَمِعَ اللّٰهُ لِمَنْ حَمِدَهٗ

رَبَّنَا لَكَ الْحَمْدُ

"Allāh listens to him who praises Him:"

"Our Lord! to Thee is due all praise."

5. Then the worshipper, saying *Allāhu Akbar*, prostrates himself, the toes of both feet, both knees, both hands, and the forehead touching the ground. This is called the *sajda* **(Illustration E)** and the following words expressing Divine greatness are uttered at least three times:

Subḥāna Rabbiya-l-ā'la.

سُبْحَانَ رَبِّيَ الْأَعْلٰى

"Glory to my Lord, the most High."

The following is an alternative form for the above-mentioned dhikr in *rukū'* or *sajda*:

Subḥāna- ka- llāhu- mma Rabba-nā wa bi-ḥamdi-ka Allāhu-mma-ghfir lī.

سُبْحَانَكَ اللّٰهُمَّ رَبَّنَا وَبِحَمْدِكَ

اَللّٰهُمَّ اغْفِرْ لِيْ

"Glory to Thee, O Allāh our Lord! and Thine is the praise; O Allāh! grant me protection."

Then, with the utterance of *Allāhu Akbar* comes the *jalsa* **(Illustration F),** a short rest in a sitting posture, the outer side of the left foot and the toes of the right one, which is in an erect position, touching the ground, and the two hands are placed on the two knees. The following prayer is offered in this condition:

Allāhu-mma ghfir-lī wa-rḥam-nī wa-hdi-ni wa 'āfi-nī wa-rzuq- nī wa-rfa-ni wa-jbur- nī.

اَللّٰهُمَّ اغْفِرْ لِيْ وَارْحَمْنِيْ وَاهْدِنِيْ

وَعَافِنِيْ وَارْزُقْنِيْ وَارْفَعْنِيْ وَاجْبُرْنِيْ

"O Allāh! grant me protection and have mercy on me and guide me and grant me security and grant me sustenance and exalt me and set right my affairs."

7. Then, with the utterance of *Allāhu Akbar* follows a second *sajda* in the same manner and with the same prayers as the first *sajda*.

The position of *sajda* is one of utmost humility and the Holy Prophet is reported to have said, "The servant is nearest to his Lord when he is in a state of *sajda*, so be frequent in your supplications to God in that condition." Any petition or any prayer to God may be made in *sajda* or in any other posture.

8. One rak'a is finished with the second sajda. The worshipper then rises, saying *Allāhu Akbar*, and assumes a standing position for the second *rak'a* and beginning with the *Fātiḥa* (p. 20 above) finishes it in the same manner as the first.

9. When the second *rak'a* is completed, the worshipper assumes a sitting posture as in *jalsa*. This is called *qa'da* **(Illustration F)**, and in this position the following prayer, called *at-ta<u>sh</u>ahhud*, is offered:

At-taḥiyyātu li-llāhī wa-ṣalawātu wa-ṭ-ṭayyibātu; as-salāmu 'alaīka ayyuha-n-Nab-īyyu wa raḥma-tu-llāhi wa barakātu-hū; as-salāmu 'alai-nā wa 'ala 'ibādillāhi-ṣ-ṣāli-ḥīn. 'A<u>sh</u>hadu allā ilāha illa-llāhu wa a<u>sh</u>hadu 'anna Muḥammadan 'abdu-hū wa rasūluh.

اَلتَّحِيَّاتُ لِلّٰهِ وَالصَّلَوٰتُ وَالطَّيِّبَاتُ
اَلسَّلَامُ عَلَيْكَ اَيُّهَا النَّبِيُّ وَرَحْمَةُ
اللّٰهِ وَبَرَكَاتُهٗ اَلسَّلَامُ عَلَيْنَا
وَعَلٰى عِبَادِ اللّٰهِ الصّٰلِحِيْنَ ۝ اَشْهَدُ
اَنْ لَّآ اِلٰهَ اِلَّا اللّٰهُ وَاَشْهَدُ اَنَّ
مُحَمَّدًا عَبْدُهٗ وَرَسُوْلُهٗ ط

"All services rendered by words and bodily actions and sacrifice of wealth are due to Allāh. Peace be on thee, O Prophet! and mercy of Allāh and His blessings. Peace be on us and on the righteous servants of Allāh. I bear witness that none deserves to be worshipped but Allāh, and I bear witness that Muḥammad is His servant and His Apostle."

The forefinger of the right hand is raised during the pronunciation of the last sentence.

10. If this is only the intermediate sitting in a prayer of three or four *rak'as*, the worshipper saying *Allāhu Akbar* stands up after the above mentioned *dhikr*, but if it is the final sitting, whether in a prayer of two or three or four *rak'as*, the following *dhikr* called *Aṣ-ṣalā 'alā-n-Nabiyy*, is added:

Allāhu-mma ṣalli 'alā Muḥammadin wa 'alā āli Muḥammadin kamā ṣallaita 'alā Ibrāhīma wa 'alā āli Ibrāhīma inna-ka Ḥamīdum Majīd. Allāhu-mma bārik 'alā Muḥammadin wa 'alā' āli Muḥammadin kamā bārakta 'alā Ibrāhīma wa 'alā' āli Ibrāhīma inna-ka Ḥamīdum-Majīd.

اَللّٰهُمَّ صَلِّ عَلٰى مُحَمَّدٍ وَّعَلٰٓى اٰلِ
مُحَمَّدٍ كَمَا صَلَّيْتَ عَلٰٓى اِبْرَاهِيْمَ
وَعَلٰٓى اٰلِ اِبْرَاهِيْمَ اِنَّكَ حَمِيْدٌ
مَّجِيْدٌ ۝ اَللّٰهُمَّ بَارِكْ عَلٰى مُحَمَّدٍ
وَّعَلٰٓى اٰلِ مُحَمَّدٍ كَمَا بَارَكْتَ عَلٰٓى
اِبْرَاهِيْمَ وَعَلٰٓى اٰلِ اِبْرَاهِيْمَ
اِنَّكَ حَمِيْدٌ مَّجِيْدٌ ۝

"O Allāh! exalt Muḥammad and the true followers of Muḥammad as Thou didst exalt Abraham and the true followers of Abraham; surely Thou art Praised, Magnified. O Allāh! bless Muḥammad and the true followers of Muḥammad as Thou didst bless Abraham and the true followers of Abraham; surely Thou art Praised, Magnified."

11. The following prayer is then added:

Rabbi-j'al-nī muqīma-ṣ-ṣalāti wa min dhurriyyatī Rabba-nā wa taqabbal du'ā; Rabba-na- ghfir-li wa li-wālidayya wa li-l-mu'minīna yauma yaqūmul-ḥisāb.

رَبِّ اجْعَلْنِيْ مُقِيْمَ الصَّلٰوةِ وَ
مِنْ ذُرِّيَّتِيْ رَبَّنَا وَتَقَبَّلْ دُعَآءِ
رَبَّنَا اغْفِرْلِيْ وَلِوَالِدَيَّ وَلِلْمُؤْمِنِيْنَ
يَوْمَ يَقُوْمُ الْحِسَابُ ۝

"My Lord! make me and my offspring keep up prayer; our Lord! and accept my prayer; our Lord! grant protection to me and my parents and to the believers on the day when the reckoning will take place."

This may be followed by any other prayer which the worshipper desires. That suitable for almost every person occurs in a ḥadīth: –

Allahu-mma inni a'ūdhu bi-ka mina-l-hammi wa-l-ḥuzni wa a'ūdhu bi-ka mina-l-'ajzi wa-l-kasali wa a'ūdhu bi-ka min-al-jubni wa-l-bukhli wa a'ūdhu bi-ka min ghalabati-d-daini wa qahri-r-rijāl; Allāhu-mma-kfi-nī bi-halāli-ka 'an harāmi-ka wa ghni-nī bi-fadzli-ka 'am-man siwā-ka.

اَللّٰهُمَّ اِنِّیْٓ اَعُوْذُ بِكَ مِنَ الْهَمِّ
وَالْحُزْنِ وَاَعُوْذُ بِكَ مِنَ الْعَجْزِ
وَالْكَسَلِ وَاَعُوْذُ بِكَ مِنَ الْجُبْنِ وَالْبُخْلِ
وَاَعُوْذُ بِكَ مِنْ غَلَبَةِ الدَّيْنِ
وَقَهْرِ الرِّجَالِ اَللّٰهُمَّ اكْفِنِیْ
بِحَلَالِكَ عَنْ حَرَامِكَ وَاَغْنِنِیْ
بِفَضْلِكَ عَمَّنْ سِوَاكَ

"O Allāh! I seek Thy refuge from anxiety and grief, and I seek Thy refuge from lack of strength and laziness, and I seek Thy refuge from cowardice and niggardliness, and I seek Thy refuge from being overpowered by debt and the oppression of men; O Allāh suffice Thou me with what is lawful, to keep me away from what is prohibited, and with Thy grace make me free from want of what is besides Thee."

12. The concluding *dhikr* in the sitting posture is *taslīm* **(Illustration G)**, or the utterance of the following words:

As-salamu 'alai-kum wa raḥmatu-llāh.

اَلسَّلَامُ عَلَيْكُمْ وَرَحْمَةُ اللّٰهِ

"Peace be on you and the mercy of Allāh!"

These words are uttered first turning the face to the right and again turning it to the left.

VIII. The *Qunūt*

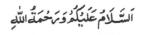

The *witr* are the three *rak'as* which are generally offered at the end of the *'Ishā* or *Tahajjud* prayers, and in the third *rak'a*

of *witr* before going to *ruku‘* or after rising from it, the following prayer, called the *Qunūt*, is offered:

Allāhu-mma-hdi-nī fi man hadaita wa ‘āfi-ni fi man ‘āfaita wa tawalla-nī fi man tawallaita wa bārik lī fi mā a‘ṭaita wa qi-nī sharra mā qadzaita inna-ka taqdzī wa lā yuqdzā ‘alai-ka, inna-hū lā yadhillu man wālaita tabārakta Rabbanā wa ta‘ālaita.

اَللّٰهُمَّ اهْدِنِيْ فِيْمَنْ هَدَيْتَ وَعَافِنِيْ
فِيْمَنْ عَافَيْتَ وَتَوَلَّنِيْ فِيْمَنْ تَوَلَّيْتَ
وَبَارِكْ لِيْ فِيْمَآ اَعْطَيْتَ وَقِنِيْ
شَرَّ مَا قَضَيْتَ اِنَّكَ تَقْضِيْ وَلَا يُقْضٰى
عَلَيْكَ اِنَّهٗ لَا يَذِلُّ مَنْ وَّالَيْتَ
تَبَارَكْتَ رَبَّنَا وَتَعَالَيْتَ

“O Allāh! guide me among those whom Thou hast guided, and preserve me among those whom Thou hast preserved, and befriend me among those whom Thou hast befriended, and bless me in what Thou hast granted and save me from the evil of what Thou has ordered, for Thou dost order and no order is given against Thy order: surely he is not disgraced whom Thou befriendest, blessed art Thou our Lord! and highly exalted.”

Another form of *Qunūt* is the following:

Allāhu-mma innā nasta‘īnu-ka, wa nastaghfiru-ka, wa nu’minu bi-ka, wa natawakkalu ‘alai-ka wa nuthnī ‘alaika-l-khaira, wa nashkuru-ka wa lā nakfuru-ka, wa nakhla‘u wa natruku man yafjuru-k; Allāhu-mma iyya-ka na‘budu wa la-ka nuṣalli wa nasjudu, wa ilai-ka nas’ā wa naḥfidu, wa narjū raḥmata-ka wa nakhshā ‘adhāba ka inna ‘adhāba ka bi-l-kuffāri mulḥiq.

اَللّٰهُمَّ اِنَّا نَسْتَعِيْنُكَ وَنَسْتَغْفِرُكَ
وَنُؤْمِنُ بِكَ وَنَتَوَكَّلُ عَلَيْكَ وَنُثْنِيْ
عَلَيْكَ الْخَيْرَ وَنَشْكُرُكَ وَلَا نَكْفُرُكَ
وَنَخْلَعُ وَنَتْرُكُ مَنْ يَّفْجُرُكَ ط
اَللّٰهُمَّ اِيَّاكَ نَعْبُدُ وَلَكَ نُصَلِّيْ
وَنَسْجُدُ وَاِلَيْكَ نَسْعٰى وَنَحْفِدُ وَ
نَرْجُوْا رَحْمَتَكَ وَنَخْشٰى عَذَابَكَ
اِنَّ عَذَابَكَ بِالْكُفَّارِ مُلْحِقٌ ط

“O Allāh! we beseech Thee for help, and seek Thy protection and believe in Thee and rely on Thee and extol Thee and are thankful to Thee and are not ungrateful to Thee and we declare ourselves clear of, and forsake, him who disobeys Thee.

"O Allāh! Thee do we serve and for Thee do we pray and prostrate ourselves, and to Thee do we betake ourselves and to obey Thee we are quick, and Thy mercy do we hope for and Thy punishment do we fear, for Thy punishment overtakes the unbelievers."

IX. ***Dhikr*** after Prayers

There is no reference in any ḥadith to the Holy Prophet raising up the hands for supplication after finishing prayers, as is the general practice, but some kinds of *dhikr* are recommended:

Astaghfiru-llāha Rabbi min kulli dhanbin wa' atūbu ilai hi.

أَسْتَغْفِرُ اللّٰهَ رَبِّي مِنْ كُلِّ ذَنْبٍ
وَّأَتُوبُ إِلَيْهِ

"I seek the protection of Allāh, my Lord, from every fault and turn to Him."

Allāhu-mma' anta-s-Salāmu wa min-ka-s-slāmu, tabārakta Rabbanā wa ta 'ālaita yā dha-l-jalāli wa-l'-ikrām.

اَللّٰهُمَّ أَنْتَ السَّلَامُ وَمِنْكَ السَّلَامُ
تَبَارَكْتَ رَبَّنَا وَتَعَالَيْتَ يَا
ذَا الْجَلَالِ وَالْإِكْرَامِ

O Allāh! Thou art the Author of peace, and from Thee comes peace; blessed art Thou, O Lord of Glory and Honour!"

Lā ilāha illa-llāhu waḥda hū lā sharīka la-hū, la-hu-l-mulku wa l-ḥamdu wa huwa 'alā kullishai'-in qadīr; Allāhu-mma lā māni'a li-mā 'a'ṭaita wa lā mu'ṭiya li-mā mana'ta wa lā yanfa'u dha-l-jaddi min-ka-l-jaddu.

لَآ إِلٰهَ إِلَّا اللّٰهُ وَحْدَهُ لَا شَرِيكَ
لَهُ لَهُ الْمُلْكُ وَالْحَمْدُ وَهُوَ عَلَى
كُلِّ شَيْءٍ قَدِيرٌ
اَللّٰهُمَّ لَا مَانِعَ لِمَا أَعْطَيْتَ وَلَا
مُعْطِيَ لِمَا مَنَعْتَ وَلَا يَنْفَعُ
ذَا الْجَدِّ مِنْكَ الْجَدُّ

"Nothing deserves to be worshipped except Allāh. He is One and has no associate; His is the kingdom and for him is praise, and He has power over all things. O Allāh! there is none who can withhold what Thou grantest, and there is none who can give what Thou withholdest, and greatness does not benefit any possessor of greatness as against Thee."

To these may be added the *āyatu-l-Kursiyy*[6] (2:255) which gives a sublime description of Divine grandeur:

Allāhu lā ilāha illā hua-al-Ḥayyu-l-Qayyūm; lā ta'khu-dhu-hū sinatun wa lā naum; la-hū mā fis-samāwāti wa mā fi-l-ardz; man dha-lladhī yashfa'u 'inda-hū illā bi idhni-hī; ya'lamu mā baina aidī-him wa mā khalfa-hum wa lā yuḥi-ṭūna bi-shai'im-min 'ilmihī illā bi-mā shā'a; wasi'a kur-siyyu-hu-s-samāwāti wa-l-ardẓ wa lā ya'ūdu-hū ḥifẓu-humā wa huwa-l-'Aliyyu-l-'Aẓim.

اَللّٰهُ لَآ اِلٰهَ اِلَّا هُوَ ۚ اَلْحَیُّ الْقَیُّوْمُ ۚ
لَا تَاْخُذُهٗ سِنَةٌ وَّلَا نَوْمٌ ؕ لَهٗ مَا فِی
السَّمٰوٰتِ وَمَا فِی الْاَرْضِ ؕ مَنْ ذَا الَّذِیْ
یَشْفَعُ عِنْدَهٗۤ اِلَّا بِاِذْنِهٖ ؕ یَعْلَمُ مَا بَیْنَ
اَیْدِیْهِمْ وَمَا خَلْفَهُمْ ۚ وَلَا یُحِیْطُوْنَ
بِشَیْءٍ مِّنْ عِلْمِهٖۤ اِلَّا بِمَا شَآءَ ۚ وَسِعَ
كُرْسِیُّهُ السَّمٰوٰتِ وَالْاَرْضَ ۚ وَلَا یَـُٔوْدُهٗ
حِفْظُهُمَا ۚ وَهُوَ الْعَلِیُّ الْعَظِیْمُ

"Allah — there is no god but He, the Ever-living, the Self-subsisting by Whom all subsist. Slumber overtakes Him not, nor sleep. To Him belongs whatever is in the heavens and whatever is in the earth. Who is he that can intercede with Him but by His permission? He knows what is before them and what is behind them. And they encompass nothing of His knowledge except what He pleases. His knowledge extends over the heavens and the earth, and the preservation of them both tires Him not. And He is the Most High, the Great."

6. The *āyatu-l-Kursiyy* may also be recited in prayers after the *Fātiḥa*.

THE FRIDAY SERVICE

There is no sabbath in Islām, and the number of prayers on Friday is the same as on any other day, with this difference that the specially ordained Friday service takes the place of the *Ẓuhr* prayer. It is the greater congregation of the Muslims at which the people of a place must all gather together, as its very name *yaum al-jumu'a* (lit. *the day of gathering*) indicates. Though all prayers are equally obligatory, yet the Holy Qur'ān has specially ordained the Friday service, and thereat it enjoins all Muslims to gather together: "O you who believe, when the call is sounded for prayer on Friday, hasten to the remembrance of Allah and leave off traffic. That is better you, if you know." (62:9). Any other prayer may be said singly under special circumstances but not so the Friday service which is essentially a congregational service. The service may be held in any mosque whether it be situated in a village or in a town or in a certain quarter of a town, or it may even be held, when necessary, in a place where there is no mosque. It is, however, true that the practice has been for all Muslims, who can do so, to gather together at a central mosque, because the underlying idea is, undoubtedly, to enable the Muslims to meet together once a week in as large a number as possible.

A special feature of the Friday service is the *khuṭba* (lit. an *address*), or a sermon, by the Imām before the prayer service is held.

Any subject relating to the welfare of the community may be dealt with in the *khuṭba*. The Holy Prophet is reported to have once prayed for rain during the sermon after somebody had directed his attention to the fact that the cattle and the people were in severe hardship on account of a drought. As regards the 'Īd *khuṭba*, it is expressly stated that the Holy Prophet used to order the raising of an army, if necessary, in the *khuṭba*, or give any other orders which he deemed necessary, in addition to admonitions of a general nature. All these facts show that the *khuṭba* is for the education of the masses, to awaken them to a general sense of duty, to lead them into the ways of their welfare and prosperity and warn them against that which is a source of loss or ruin to them. Therefore the *khuṭba* must be delivered in a language which the people understand and there is no sense in delivering it in Arabic to an audience which does not know that language. Divine service is quite a different thing from the sermon. The sermon is meant to exhort the people, to give them information as to what to do under certain circumstances and what not to do; it is meant, in fact, to throw light on all questions of life; and to understand a sermon in a foreign language requires an extensive, almost an exhaustive, knowledge of that language. Not so in the case of Divine service, which consists of a number of stated sentences and the meaning of which can be fully understood even by a child, in one month. Moreover, in Divine service the different postures of the body are in themselves expressive of Divine praise and glory, even if the worshipper does not understand the significance of the words. It is, therefore, of the utmost importance that the masses should know what the preacher is saying. In fact, the Friday sermon is the best means of education for the masses and for maintaining the vitality of the Muslim community as a whole.

After the first *Adhān* is called, those gathered say the Sunnah prayers, (2 rak'as); even if a person comes late and the Imam has already started the sermon, the late comer must still perform these two rak'as. The *Mu'adhdhin* then calls the second *Adhān*. The *Imām* then stands up facing the congregation and delivers the *khuṭba*. He begins with the *Kalima shahāda* in the following words:

اَشْهَدُ اَنْ لَّآ اِلٰهَ اِلَّا اللّٰهُ
وَحْدَهٗ لَا شَرِيْكَ لَهٗ وَاَشْهَدُ
اَنَّ مُحَمَّدًا عَبْدُهٗ وَرَسُوْلُهٗ
اَمَّا بَعْدُ فَاَعُوْذُ بِاللّٰهِ مِنَ
الشَّيْطٰنِ الرَّجِيْمِ بِسْمِ اللّٰهِ
الرَّحْمٰنِ الرَّحِيْمِ

Ash-ha-du al-lā ilāha illa-llāhu waḥda-hu-lā-sharīka lahu wa ashhadu anna Muhammadan abduhu wa rasulu-hu; ammā ba'du fa 'a'ūzu billā-hi minash-shāiṭān-irrajīm. Bismillā-hir-Rahmān nir-Rahīm.

"I bear witness that nothing deserves to be worshipped except Allah Who has no partners and I bear witness that

Muhammad is His servant and messenger. After this I seek refuge in Allāh from the accursed devil. I begin in the name of Allāh, the Beneficent, the Merciful."

The *Imam* then recites a Qur'anic text on which he wants to address the congregation, who are especially enjoined to remain sitting and silent during the *Khutba*. The *Khutba* is delivered in two parts. The *Imam* after finishing the address, breaks the sermon by a short interval during which he sits down. Then standing again he continues and completes the Khutba. The following are some of the more common prayers recited in this in this portion:[7]

Al-ḥamdu li-llāhi naḥ madu-hū wa nasta'īnu-hū wa nastaghfi ru-hū wa numinu bi hi wa na tawakklu 'alai hi wa na'ūdhu bi-llāhi min shurūri anfusi-nā wa min sayyi'āti a'mālinā, man yahdi-hi-llāhu fa-lā mudzilla la-hū wa man yudzlilhu fa-lā hādiya-la hū. Allāhum-man-ṣur man-naṣara dīna Muhammadin ṣal-lallā-hu alai-hi wa sallama waj-al nā-min-hum. Allāhum-makhzul man khazala dinu Muhammadin ṣal-lallā-hu alai-hi wa sallam wa lā taj-'alnā min hum.

اَلْحَمْدُ لِلّٰهِ نَحْمَدُهٗ وَنَسْتَعِيْنُهٗ وَ
نَسْتَغْفِرُهٗ وَنُؤْمِنُ بِهٖ وَنَتَوَكَّلُ
عَلَيْهِ وَنَعُوْذُ بِاللّٰهِ مِنْ شُرُوْرِ
اَنْفُسِنَا وَمِنْ سَيِّاٰتِ اَعْمَالِنَا مَنْ
يَّهْدِهِ اللّٰهُ فَلَا مُضِلَّ لَهٗ وَمَنْ
يُّضْلِلْهُ فَلَا هَادِيَ لَهٗ اَللّٰهُمَّ انْصُرْ
مَنْ نَّصَرَ دِيْنَ مُحَمَّدٍ صَلَّى اللّٰهُ
عَلَيْهِ وَسَلَّمَ وَاجْعَلْنَا مِنْهُمْ اَللّٰهُمَّ
اخْذُلْ مَنْ خَذَلَ دِيْنَ مُحَمَّدٍ صَلَّى
اللّٰهُ عَلَيْهِ وَسَلَّمَ وَلَا تَجْعَلْنَا مِنْهُمْ

"All praise is due to Allāh; we praise Him and we beseech Him for help and we ask for His protection and we seek refuge in Allāh from the mischiefs of our souls, and from the evil of our deeds; whomsoever Allāh guides, there is none who can lead him astray and whom Allāh finds in error, there is none to guide him. O Allāh! help those who help the religion of Muhammad (the peace and blessings of Allāh be upon him!) and count us among them. O Allāh! disappoint those who try to disgrace the religion of Muhammad (peace and blessings of Allāh be upon him) and do not make us of those."

7. These prayers are being inserted by the Publisher.

The *Imam* then recites the *Durud* or *al-ṣalā ʻalā-Nabiyy* (page 24) and then the following Qur'anic verse (16:90):

Inn-al lā-ha ya'mu-ru bil-ad-li wal'ih-sān-ni wa'ī-t'i,-zil qur-bā wa yan-hā ʻa-nil fah-shā'i wal-mun-ka-ri wal bagh-yi ya-ʻi-ẓu-kum laʻal-la-kum ta-zak-ka-rūn.

إِنَّ اللّٰهَ يَأْمُرُ بِالْعَدْلِ وَالْإِحْسَانِ
وَإِيْتَآئِ ذِي الْقُرْبٰى وَيَنْهٰى عَنِ
الْفَحْشَآءِ وَالْمُنْكَرِ وَالْبَغْيِ يَعِظُكُمْ
لَعَلَّكُمْ تَذَكَّرُوْنَ ۝

ʻI-bā-dal lā-hi uzku-rul lāh-ha yaz-kur kum wad-ʻu-hu yas-ta-jib la-kum wa-la-dhik-rul lā-hi ak-bar.

عِبَادَ اللّٰهِ اذْكُرُوا اللّٰهَ يَذْكُرْكُمْ
وَادْعُوْهُ يَسْتَجِبْ لَكُمْ وَلَذِكْرُ
اللّٰهِ أَكْبَرُ ط

"Surely Allāh enjoins the doing of justice and the doing of good (to others) and the giving to the kindred, and He forbids indecency and evil and rebellion. He admonishes you that you may be mindful."

"O servants of Allāh, remember Allāh. He will remember you; call on Him. He will answer your call. And verily remembrance of Allāh is greater than everything."

After the sermon is finished, the *iqāma* is pronounced and a congregational service of two rakʻas is held, in which the Imām recites the *Fātiḥa* and a portion of the Qur'ān in a loud voice, as he does in the morning and evening prayers. This is the only obligatory service. Two *rakʻas* (*sunna*) are said after the service has been finished. There is not the least authority for saying *Ẓuhr* prayer[8] after the Friday service, which in fact takes the place of *Ẓuhr* prayers.

THE ʻĪD PRAYERS

There are, in Islām, two great festivals having a religious sanction, and in connection with both of them a congregational service of two *rakʻas* is held, followed by a *khuṭba* or sermon.

8. The origin of this practice is in the wrong impression that Friday service can only be held in a city or under the Muslim rule. As a matter of fact, as already shown, it may be held in a city or in a village or anywhere else. So also the condition that it can only be held under Muslim rule is simply absurd. The Qur'ān and the Ḥadith place no such limitation on the Friday service or on any other service.

Both these festivals go under the name of *ʻĪd* which means *a recurring happiness*, being derived from *ʻaud* meaning *to return*. The first of these is called the *ʻĪd al-Fiṭr*, and it follows ramadān, the month of fasting, and takes place on the first of Shawwāl. The other is *ʻĪd al-Adzḥā* and it takes place on the 10th of Dhu-l-Ḥijja, the day following the day of pilgrimage.

The preparation for *ʻĪd* is similar to the preparation for the Friday service. One must take a bath, put on one's best clothes, use scent, and do everything possible to appear neat and tidy. The gathering in the *ʻĪd* should preferably be in an open place, but, if necessary, a mosque may also be used for holding the Divine service. An open space is preferable on account of the size of the congregation, which a mosque might not be able to hold. No *adhān* is called out for the *ʻĪd* prayers nor an *iqāma* for the arranging of the lines. Though women take part in all the prayers and in the Friday service, they are specially enjoined to be present at the *ʻĪd* gatherings, for the Holy Prophet is reported to have said "the young girls and those that have taken to seclusion and those that have their menses on, should all go out (for the *ʻĪd*) and be present at the prayers of the Muslims." The time of *ʻĪd* prayers is any time after sunrise and before noon.

The *ʻĪd* service consists only of two *rakʻas* in congregation. The Imām recites the *Fātiḥa* and a portion of the Holy Qur'ān in a loud voice, as in the Friday service. As already noted, there is neither *adhān* nor *iqāma* for the *ʻĪd* prayer, but there is a number of *takbīrs*[9] in addition to those that are meant to indicate the changes of position. On the best authority, the number of these additional *takbīrs* is seven in the first *rakʻa* and five in the second, before the recital of the *Fātiḥa* in both *rakʻas*.[10] The *takbīrs* are uttered aloud by the Imām one after another as he raises both hands to the ears and then leaves them free in the natural position. Those who stand behind him raise and lower their hands similarly.

9. The calling aloud of *Allāhu Akbar*.

10. As stated above, the number of additional *takbīrs* given here is on the best authority available. A difference of opinion does, however, exist on this point. But much importance should not be attached to these matters. Some people say four additional *takbīrs* in the first *rakʻa* and three in the second, in the latter case before going to *rukūʻ*. The ḥadīth, however, on which this is based, is not reliable.

The *'Īd* sermon is delivered after the Divine service is over. As regards the manner and the subject dealt with, it is similar to the Friday sermon, except that it is not necessary to break it up into two parts by assuming the sitting posture in the middle of it. It was the Holy Prophet's practice to address the women separately, who were all required to be present whether they joined the service or not.

While celebrating the great *'Īd* festivals, a Muslim not only remembers God (by attending the service) but he is also enjoined to remember his poorer brethren. The institution of a charitable fund is associated with both *'Īds*. On the occasion of the *'Īd al-Fiṭr*, every Muslim is required to give *ṣadaqa Fiṭr* (lit. *the Fiṭr charity*) which amounts to three or four seers of wheat, barley, rice or any other staple food of the country, per head of the family, including the old as well as the youngest members, males as well as females.

The payment is to be made before the service is held, and it is obligatory *(fardz)*. Like *zakāt*, the *Fiṭr* charity was an organized institution, as expressly mentioned in a ḥadīth: "They gave this charity to be gathered together, and it was not given away to beggars."

The principle of gathering the *Fiṭr* charity has now been abandoned by the Muslims, and the result is that a most beneficial institution of Islām for the upliftment of the poor and needy has been thrown into neglect, and the money which could strengthen national funds is merely wasted.

'Īd al-Adzḥā also furnishes an occasion for the exercise of charity. Every Muslim who has the means is required to sacrifice an animal[10] after the prayers are over, and this not only makes the poorest members of the community enjoy the festival with a good feast of meat, but national funds for the amelioration of the poor or the welfare of the community, can be considerably strengthened if the skins of the sacrificed animals are devoted to this purpose. In addition to this, in places where the numbers of sacrificed animals is in excess of the needs of the population, the surplus may be refrigerated or dried and sold, and the proceeds thereof used for some charitable object.

11. One goat or one sheep suffices for one household; in the case of a cow or a camel, seven men may be partners.

The *Tahajjud* prayer which is said during the latter half of the night consists of eight *rak'as* divided into a service of two at a time, followed by three *rak'as* of *witr*. To make it easier for the common people, *witr* prayer, which is really a part of *Tahajjud*, has been made a part of *'Ishā* or night prayer, and therefore, if the *witr* prayer has been said with *'Ishā*, *Tahajjud* would consist of only eight *rak'as*. But if there is not sufficient time, one may stop after any two *rak'as*. The Holy Prophet laid special stress on *Tahajjud* in the month of Ramadzān, and it was the *Tahajjud* prayer that ultimately took the form of *Tarāwīḥ* in that month. The Companions of the Holy Prophet were very particular about *Tahajjud* prayer, though they knew that it was not obligatory, and some of them used to come to the mosque during the latter part of the night to say their *Tahajjud* prayers. It is reported that the Holy Prophet had a small closet made for himself in the mosque and furnished with a mat as a place of seclusion wherein to say his *Tahajjud* prayers during the month of Ramadzān, and on a certain night, when he rose up to say his *Tahajjud* prayers, some people who were in the mosque saw him and followed him in prayer, thus making a congregation. On the following night, this congregation increased, and swelled to still larger numbers on the third. On the fourth night the Holy Prophet did not come out, saying he feared lest it be made obligatory and that it was preferable to say the *Tahajjud* prayers in one's own house. *Tahajjud*, except for these three days, thus remained an individual prayer during the lifetime of the Holy Prophet, the caliphate of Abu Bakr, and the early part of the caliphate of 'Umar. But later on, 'Umar introduced a change whereby this prayer became a congregational prayer during the early part of the night, and was said after the *'Ishā* prayer and this prayer has received the name of *Tarāwīḥ*.

It is now the practice that the whole of the Holy Qur'ān is recited in the *Tarāwīḥ* prayers in the month of Ramadzān. But to recite it in a single night is against the express injunctions of the Holy Prophet. The number of *rak'as* in the *Tarāwīḥ* prayers seems, at first, to have been eleven, being exactly the number of *rak'as* in the *Tahajjud* prayers (including of course three *witr rak'as*). It is stated that 'Umar at first ordered eleven *rak'as*, but later on the number seems to have been increased to twenty *rak'as* of *Tarāwīḥ* and three *rak'as* of *witr,* making a total of twenty-three.

Prayer or Service for Rain

It is reported that on a certain occasion when there had been a long drought, someone requested the Holy Prophet, while he was delivering the Friday sermon in the mosque, to pray for rain, as both men and cattle were suffering severely, and in response, the Prophet raised his hands and prayed to God for rain.

Similarly he is reported to have prayed to God when there was excess of rain. On another occasion, however, he is said to have gone out into the open with the congregation, and to have prayed for rain and then performed two *rak'as* of prayer in congregation, reading the *Fātiḥa* in a loud voice, as in the Friday service.

Service During Eclipse

A prayer service of two *rak'as* was held by the Holy Prophet during an eclipse of the sun. The service differed from the ordinary prayer service in that there were two *qiyāms* and two *rukū's* in each *rak'a.*

After the first *qiyām* there was a *rukū'* as in the ordinary service, though of a longer duration, and then a *qiyām* followed again in which a portion of the Holy Qur'ān was recited; this was followed by a second *rukū'*, after rising from which, the *sajda* was performed as in the ordinary service; the recitation being in a loud voice, as in the Friday and *'Īd* prayers. There is also mention of a *khuṭba* (sermon) having been delivered after the service.

Service on the Dead

A Divine service is held over the dead body of every Muslim, young or old, even of infants who have lived only for a few minutes or seconds. When a person dies, the body is washed with soap or some other disinfectant and cleansed of all impurities which may be due to disease. In washing the dead body, the parts which are washed in *wuḏẕū* are taken first, and then the whole body is washed. It is then wrapped in one or more white sheets, and scent is also added. In the case of martyrs, or persons slain in battle, the washing and wrapping in white cloth is dispensed with. The dead body is then placed on a bier or, if necessary, in a coffin, and carried on the shoulders to its last resting-place as a mark of respect; though the carrying of the body by any other means is not prohibited. The Holy Prophet stood up when he saw the bier of a Jew pass by. This he did to show respect to the dead, and then enjoined his followers to stand up as a mark of respect when a bier passed by, whether it was that of a Muslim or a non-Muslim.

Following the dead body to the grave and taking part in the Divine service held over it is regarded as a duty which a Muslim owes to a Muslim, and so is also the visiting of the sick. Technically, taking part in Divine service is called *fardz kifāya,* which means that it is sufficient that some Muslims should take part in it. Women are not prohibited from going with the bier, though their presence is not considered desirable, because being more tender-hearted than men, they may break down by reason of their grief. The service may be held anywhere, in a mosque or in an open space or even in the graveyard if sufficient ground is available there. All those who take part in the service must perform *wuḏẕū* (see p. 6). The bier is placed in front; the Imām stands facing the middle of the bier and the people form themselves into lines according to the number of those who take part, facing the Qibla. The general practice is to have three lines at least. If the number of people is very small, there is no harm if they form only a single line.

The service starts with the *takbīr* (saying *Allāhu Akbar*), with the pronouncement of which hands are raised to the ears and placed in the same position as in prayer (see p. 11). After the *takbīr, istiftāḥ* (see p. 11) and the *Fātiḥa* (see p. 20) are recited in a low voice by the Imām as well as those who follow. Then follows a second *takbīr* without raising the hands to the ears, and the *dhikr* known as *aṣ-ṣalā 'alā Nabiyy* (see p. 24) is recited in a low voice. The third *takbīr* is then pronounced in a manner similar to the second *takbīr,* and a prayer for the forgiveness of the deceased is addressed to God. Different forms of this prayer are reported as having been offered by the Holy Prophet, and it seems that prayer in any form is permissible.

The following is the most well known:

اَللّٰهُمَّ اغْفِرْ لِحَيِّنَا وَمَيِّتِنَا وَشَاهِدِنَا
وَغَائِبِنَا وَصَغِيْرِنَا وَكَبِيْرِنَا وَذَكَرِنَا
وَاُنْثَانَا اَللّٰهُمَّ مَنْ اَحْيَيْتَهٗ مِنَّا
فَاَحْيِهٖ عَلَى الْاِسْلَامِ وَمَنْ تَوَفَّيْتَهٗ
مِنَّا فَتَوَفَّهٗ عَلَى الْاِيْمَانِ
اَللّٰهُمَّ لَا تَحْرِمْنَا اَجْرَهٗ
وَلَا تَفْتِنَّا بَعْدَهٗ

Allāh-umma-ghfir li-ḥayyi-nā wa mayyiti-nā wa shāhidi-nā wa ghā-'ibi-nā wa ṣaghīri-na wa kabīri-nā wa dhakari-nā wa unthā-nā; Allāh-umma man aḥyaita-hū minnā fa-aḥyi hī 'ala-l-Islāmi wa man tawaffaita-hū minnā fatawaffa-hū 'ala-l-īmāni; Allāh-umma lā taḥrim-nā ajra-hū wa lā taftin-nā ba'da-hū.

"O Allāh! grant protection to our living and to our dead and to those of us who are present and those who are absent, and to our young and our old folk and to our males and our females; O Allāh! whomsoever Thou grantest to live from among us, cause him to live in Islām (submission) and whomsoever of us Thou causest to die, make him die in faith; O Allāh! do not deprive us of his reward and do not make us fall into a trial after him."

Another prayer runs thus:

اَللّٰهُمَّ اغْفِرْ لَهٗ وَارْحَمْهُ وَعَافِهٖ
وَاعْفُ عَنْهُ وَاَكْرِمْ نُزُلَهٗ وَوَسِّعْ
مَدْخَلَهٗ وَاغْسِلْهُ بِالْمَآءِ وَالثَّلْجِ

Allāh-umma ghfir la-hū wa-rḥam-hu wa 'āfi-hi wa-'fu 'an-hu wa akrim nuzula-hū wa wassi' madkhala-hū waghsil-hu bi-l-mā'i wa-th-thalji wa-l-baradi wa naqqi-hī mina-l-khaṭāyā kamā naqqaita-th-thauba-l-abyadza mina-d-danasi.

وَالْبَرَدِ وَنَقِّهِ مِنَ الْخَطَايَا
كَمَا نَقَّيْتَ الثَّوْبَ الْأَبْيَضَ
مِنَ الدَّنَسِ

"O Allāh! grant him protection, and have mercy on him, and keep him in good condition, and pardon him, and make his entertainment honourable, and expand his place of entering, and wash him with water and snow and hail and clean him of faults as the white cloth is cleansed of dross."

The prayers for the deceased are followed by a fourth *takbīr,* after which comes the *taslīm* as at the close of prayers (see p. 25). A similar Divine service may be held in the case of a dead man when the dead body is not present. When the service is finished, the bier is taken to the grave and buried. The grave is dug in such a manner that the dead body may be laid in it facing Makka. It is generally between four and six feet deep, and an oblong excavation is made on one side, wherein the dead body is to be placed. This is called the *laḥd.* The dead body is made to rest in the *laḥd* facing the Qibla. If the dead body is contained in a coffin, the *laḥd* may be dispensed with. The following words are reported in a ḥadīth as having been uttered by the Holy Prophet when placing a dead body in the grave:

Bi-smi-llāhi wa bi-llāhi wa 'alā sunnati Rasūli-llāh.

بِسْمِ اللّٰهِ وَبِاللّٰهِ وَعَلٰى سُنَّةِ
رَسُوْلِ اللّٰهِ

"In the name of Allāh and with Allāh and according to the sunna of the Messenger of Allāh."

The grave is then filled in and a prayer is again offered for the dead one and the people then depart. The funeral service of a child is similar to that of one who has reached the age of discretion, except that in the prayer after the third *takbīr* the following words are recited:

Allāhu-mma-j'al-hu la-nā faraṭan wa salafan wa ajran.

اَللّٰهُمَّ اجْعَلْهُ لَنَا فَرَطًا وَّسَلَفًا
وَّاَجْرًا

"O Allāh! make him for us a cause of recompense in the world to come and as one going before and a treasure and a reward."

Birth Rites

The formalities that are required at the birth of a child are very few. The most important of these is the calling out of *adhān* (for which see p. 6) in a low voice in the right ear and the calling out of *iqāma* (for which see p. 10) in the left ear of the new-born infant. The hair of the head is shaved off on the eighth day after birth and at the same time, if the parents can afford, one goat is sacrificed in the case of a daughter and two in that of a son, the flesh being distributed among relatives and friends. This is called *'aqīqa.* Circumcision or the removal of foreskin is resorted to in the case of a boy preferably at an early date. The practice of circumcision dates back to the days of Abraham and is now recognized by medical opinion as a remedy for many diseases.

Marriage Sermon

According to the Islamic law marriage is a sacred contract between the husband and the wife; it is expressly called a covenant in the Holy Qur'ān (4:21). A contract can only be made by the consent of the two contracting parties and it is necessary that the husband and the wife should "agree among themselves in a lawful manner" (2:232). Hence the first requisite of marriage is that each party should satisfy itself as to the desirability of choosing the other as a partner in life.

The second requisite of marriage is that the husband should settle a dowry (called the *mahr*) on the wife. It is described as "a free gift" from the husband to the wife given at the time of marriage (4:4). The amount of dowry depends upon the circumstances of the husband and the position of the wife. No limit is placed upon the *mahr.* It may be as low as a ring of iron according to a ḥadīth, and it may be as high as a heap of gold according to the Holy Qur'ān (4:20).

The third requisite of marriage is a public announcement

relating to it, attended with the delivery of a *khuṭba* (sermon) which gives the marriage a sacred character. The sermon should begin with *tashahhud* which runs as follows:

Al-ḥamdu li-llāhi naḥmadu-hū wa nasta'īnu-hū wa nastaghfiru-hū wa na'ūdhu bi-llāhi min shurūri anfusi-nā wa min sayyi'āti a'mālinā, man yahdi-hi-llāhu fa-lā mudzilla la-hū wa man yudzlil hu fa-lā hādiya-la-hū; ashhadu al lā ilāha illa-llāhu wa ashhadu anna Muḥammadan 'abdu-hu wa Rasulu-hu.

اَلْحَمْدُ لِلّٰهِ نَحْمَدُهٗ وَنَسْتَعِيْنُهٗ
وَنَسْتَغْفِرُهٗ وَنَعُوْذُ بِاللّٰهِ مِنْ
شُرُوْرِ اَنْفُسِنَا وَمِنْ سَيِّاٰتِ
اَعْمَالِنَا وَمَنْ يَّهْدِهِ اللّٰهُ فَلَا مُضِلَّ
لَهٗ وَمَنْ يُّضْلِلْهُ فَلَا هَادِيَ لَهٗ
اَشْهَدُ اَنْ لَّآ اِلٰهَ اِلَّا اللّٰهُ وَاَشْهَدُ
اَنَّ مُحَمَّدًا عَبْدُهٗ وَرَسُوْلُهٗ

All praise is due to Allāh; we praise Him and we beseech Him for help and we ask for His protection and we seek refuge in Allāh from the mischiefs of our souls, and from the evil of our deeds; whomsoever Allāh guides, there is none who can lead him astray and whom Allāh finds in error, there is none to guide him; I bear witness that there is no god but Allāh and that Muḥammad is His servant and His Messenger."

After the *tashahhud,* the following four verses of the Holy Qur'ān are recited, *viz.* 3:102; 4:1; 33:70, 71. These verses remind man of his responsibilities in general, and the middle one lays particular stress on the obligations towards women. They run as follows:

Yā ayyuha-lladhīna āmanu-ttaqu-llāha ḥaqqa tuqāti-hi wa lā tamūtunna illā wa antum Muslimūn.

يٰۤاَيُّهَا الَّذِيْنَ اٰمَنُوا اتَّقُوا اللّٰهَ حَقَّ
تُقٰتِهٖ وَلَا تَمُوْتُنَّ اِلَّا وَاَنْتُمْ
مُّسْلِمُوْنَ ۝

"O you who believe, keep your duty to Allah as it ought to be kept, and die not unless you are Muslims."

يٰٓاَيُّهَا النَّاسُ اتَّقُوْا رَبَّكُمُ الَّذِيْ
خَلَقَكُمْ مِّنْ نَّفْسٍ وَّاحِدَةٍ
وَّخَلَقَ مِنْهَا زَوْجَهَا وَبَثَّ
مِنْهُمَا رِجَالًا كَثِيْرًا وَّنِسَآءً ۚ
وَاتَّقُوا اللّٰهَ الَّذِيْ تَسَآءَلُوْنَ
بِهٖ وَالْاَرْحَامَ ۭ اِنَّ اللّٰهَ كَانَ
عَلَيْكُمْ رَقِيْبًا ۝

Yā ayyuha- n- nāsu- ttaqū Rabba-kumu-lladhi khalaqa-kum min nafsin wāḥidatin wa khalaqa min hā zauja-hā wa baththa min humā rijālan kathīran wa nisā'a; wattaqu llāha-lladhī tasā'alūna bi-hī wa-l-arḥām; inna-llāha kāna 'alai-kum raqībā.

"O people, keep your duty to your Lord, Who created you from a single being and created its mate of the same (kind), and spread from these two many men and women. And keep your duty to Allah, by Whom you demand one of another (your rights), and (to) the ties of relationship. Surely Allah is ever a Watcher over you."

يٰٓاَيُّهَا الَّذِيْنَ اٰمَنُوا اتَّقُوا اللّٰهَ وَقُوْلُوْا
قَوْلًا سَدِيْدًا ۝ يُّصْلِحْ لَكُمْ اَعْمَالَكُمْ
وَيَغْفِرْ لَكُمْ ذُنُوْبَكُمْ ۭ وَمَنْ يُّطِعِ
اللّٰهَ وَرَسُوْلَهٗ فَقَدْ فَازَ فَوْزًا
عَظِيْمًا ۝

Yā ayyuha-lladhīna āmanu-ttaqu-llāha wa qūlū qaulan sadīdan yuṣliḥ la-kum a'māla-kum wa yaghfir la-kum dhunūba-kum wa man yuṭi'i-llāha wa Rasūla-hū fa-qad fāza fauzan 'aẓīmā.

"O you who believe, keep your duty to Allah and speak straight words: He will put your deeds into a right state for you, and forgive you your sins. And whoever obeys Allah and His Messenger, he indeed achieves a mighty success."

The sermon of course must expatiate on these verses and explain to the audience the mutual rights and duties of husband and wife. At the conclusion of the sermon is made the announcement that such and such a man and such and such a woman have accepted each other as husband and wife, and the dowry is also announced at the time.

The man and the woman are then asked if they accept this new relationship, and on the reply being given in the affirmative, the marriage ceremony proper is concluded. In India the consent of the woman is generally obtained through her father or other guardian or relation. After the expression of consent by both parties, the whole audience raises its hands and prays for the blessings of God on the newly wedded couple. The words of the prayer as reported in Ḥadith are:

Bāraka-llāhu wa bāraka 'alaika wa jama'a baina-kumā bi-l-khair.	بَارَكَ اللّٰهُ وَبَارَكَ عَلَيْكَ وَ جَمَعَ بَيْنَكُمَا بِالْخَيْرِ

"May Allāh shower His blessings and may He bless you and unite you two in goodness."

To this may be added any other prayer for the welfare and prosperity of the couple, or prayers of a general nature for the welfare of all. Generally dates or sweets are distributed before the audience disperses. The marriage is generally followed by a feast called the *walīma.*

Slaughtering of Animals

All animals that are allowed as food, excepting fish and other water-game, must be slaughtered in such a manner that blood flows out, and the following words should be pronounced at the time of slaughtering: *Bi-smi llāhi Allāhu Akbar,* i.e., "In the name of Allāh — Allāh is the Greatest."

Quranic Prayers

Below are given some of the prayers which are met with in the Holy Qur'ān. They can serve a general purpose as well as the purpose of recitation in prayers after the *Fātiḥa* (see p. 21 where it is stated that the recitation of the *Fātiḥa* should be followed by a recitation of any portion of the Holy Qur'ān). Some of them are for particular occasions as indicated by the words:

رَبَّنَآ اٰتِنَا فِي الدُّنْيَا حَسَنَةً وَّ
فِي الْاٰخِرَةِ حَسَنَةً وَّقِنَا عَذَابَ
النَّارِ

Rabba-nā āti-na fi-d-dunyā ḥasanatan wa fi-l ākhirati ḥasantan wa qi-nā 'adhāba-n-nār.

"Our Lord! grant us good in this world and good in the hereafter and save us from the chastisement of the fire" (2:201).

رَبَّنَآ اَفْرِغْ عَلَيْنَا صَبْرًا وَّثَبِّتْ
اَقْدَامَنَا وَانْصُرْنَا عَلَى الْقَوْمِ
الْكٰفِرِيْنَ

Rabba-nā afrigh 'alai-nā ṣabran wa thabbit aqdāma-nā wa-nṣur-nā 'ala-l-qaumi-l-kafirīn.

"Our Lord, pour out patience on us and make our steps firm and help us against the disbelieving people." (2:250).

رَبَّنَا لَا تُؤَاخِذْنَآ اِنْ نَّسِيْنَآ
اَوْ اَخْطَاْنَا ۚ رَبَّنَا وَلَا تَحْمِلْ عَلَيْنَآ
اِصْرًا كَمَا حَمَلْتَهٗ عَلَى الَّذِيْنَ مِنْ
قَبْلِنَا ۚ رَبَّنَا وَلَا تُحَمِّلْنَا مَا لَا
طَاقَةَ لَنَا بِهٖ ۚ وَاعْفُ عَنَّا
وَاغْفِرْ لَنَا وَارْحَمْنَا اَنْتَ مَوْلٰىنَا
فَانْصُرْنَا عَلَى الْقَوْمِ الْكٰفِرِيْنَ

Rabba-nā lā tu'ākhidh-nā in-nasī-nā au akhta'nā, Rabba-nā wa lā taḥmil 'alai-nā iṣran kamā ḥamalta-hū 'ala-lladhī na min qabli-nā, Rabba-nā wa lā tuḥammil-nā mā lā ṭāqata la-nā bih; wa-'fu 'an-nā wa ghfir la-nā wa-rḥam-nā anta Maulā-nā fa-nṣur nā 'ala-l-qaumi-l-kāfirīn.

"Our Lord, punish us not if we forget or make a mistake. Our Lord, do not lay on us a burden as Thou didst lay on those before us. Our Lord, impose not on us (afflictions) which we have not the strength to bear. And pardon us! And grant us protection! And have mercy on us! Thou art our Patron, so grant us victory over the disbelieving people." (2:286).

رَبَّنَا لَا تُزِغْ قُلُوْبَنَا بَعْدَ اِذْ
هَدَيْتَنَا وَهَبْ لَنَا مِنْ لَّدُنْكَ
رَحْمَةً ۚ اِنَّكَ اَنْتَ الْوَهَّابُ

Rabba-nā lā tuzigh qulūba-nā ba'da idh hadaita-nā wa hab la-nā mil ladun-ka raḥma, inna-ka anta-l-Wahhāb.

"Our Lord! do not make our hearts deviate after Thou hast guided us aright and grant us from Thee mercy: surely Thou art the most liberal Giver" (3:8).

رَبِّ هَبْ لِي مِنْ لَّدُنْكَ ذُرِّيَّةً
طَيِّبَةً ۚ إِنَّكَ سَمِيعُ الدُّعَاءِ

Rabbi hab lī mil-ladun-ka dhur-riyyatan ṭayyiba, inna ka Samī' ud-du'ā.

"My Lord! grant me from Thee goodly offspring; surely Thou art the Hearer of prayer" (3:38).

رَبَّنَا اغْفِرْ لَنَا ذُنُوبَنَا وَإِسْرَافَنَا
فِي أَمْرِنَا وَثَبِّتْ أَقْدَامَنَا
وَانْصُرْنَا عَلَى الْقَوْمِ الْكَافِرِينَ

Rabba-na-ghfir la-nā dhunūba-nā wa isrāfa-nā fī amri-nā wa thabbit aqdāma-nā wa nṣur-nā 'ala-l-qaumi-l-kāfirīn.

"Our Lord, grant us protection from our sins and our extravagance in our affair, and make firm our feet and grant us victory over the disbelieving people." (3:147).

رَبَّنَا إِنَّنَا سَمِعْنَا مُنَادِيًا يُنَادِي
لِلْإِيمَانِ أَنْ آمِنُوا بِرَبِّكُمْ فَآمَنَّا
رَبَّنَا فَاغْفِرْ لَنَا ذُنُوبَنَا وَكَفِّرْ عَنَّا
سَيِّئَاتِنَا وَتَوَفَّنَا مَعَ الْأَبْرَارِ
رَبَّنَا وَآتِنَا مَا وَعَدْتَنَا عَلَىٰ
رُسُلِكَ وَلَا تُخْزِنَا يَوْمَ الْقِيَامَةِ
إِنَّكَ لَا تُخْلِفُ الْمِيعَادَ

Rabba-nā inna-nā sami'-nā munā diyan yunādī li-l-īmāni an āminū bi-Rabbi-kum fa āmannā, Rabbanā fa-ghfir la -nā dhunūba-nā wa kaffir 'an-nā sayyi'āti-nā wa tawaffa-nā ma'a-l-abrār. Rabba-nā wa āti-nā mā wa'adta-na 'alā rusuli-ka wa lā tukhzi-nā yauma-l-qiyāmati inna-ka lā tukhlifu-l-mī'ad.

"Our Lord, surely we have heard a Crier calling to the faith, saying: Believe in your Lord. So we do believe. Our Lord, grant us protection from our sins and remove our evils and make us die with the righteous. Our Lord, grant us what Thou hast promised us by Thy messengers and disgrace us not on the day of Resurrection. Surely Thou never failest in (Thy) promise!" (3:193, 194).

Rabba-na a<u>kh</u>rij-nā min hā<u>dh</u>i-hi-l-qaryat-iẓ-ẓālimi ahlu hā wa j'al la-nā mil-ladun-ka waliyyan wa-j'al la-nā mil-ladun-ka naṣīrā.

رَبَّنَآ أَخْرِجْنَا مِنْ هٰذِهِ الْقَرْيَةِ
الظَّالِمِ أَهْلُهَا وَاجْعَلْ لَّنَا مِنْ لَّدُنْكَ
وَلِيًّا ۚ وَّاجْعَلْ لَّنَا مِنْ لَّدُنْكَ نَصِيْرًا

"Our Lord, take us out of this town, whose people are oppressors, and grant us from Thee a friend, and grant us from Thee a helper!" (4:75).

Rabba-nā ẓalamnā anfusa-nā wa il lam ta<u>gh</u>fir la-nā wa tarḥam-na la-nakūnanna mina-l-<u>kh</u>āsirīn.

رَبَّنَا ظَلَمْنَآ أَنْفُسَنَا وَإِنْ لَّمْ تَغْفِرْ لَنَا
وَتَرْحَمْنَا لَنَكُوْنَنَّ مِنَ الْخٰسِرِيْنَ

"Our Lord, we have wronged ourselves; and if Thou forgive us not, and have (not) mercy on us, we shall certainly be of the losers." (7:23).

Rabba-na-ftaḥ baina nā wa baina qaumi-nā bi-l-ḥaqqi wa anta <u>Kh</u>airu-l-fātiḥīn.

رَبَّنَا افْتَحْ بَيْنَنَا وَبَيْنَ قَوْمِنَا
بِالْحَقِّ وَأَنْتَ خَيْرُ الْفٰتِحِيْنَ

"Our Lord! decide between us and our people with truth; and Thou art the Best of Deciders" (7:89).

Rabba-nā lā taj'al-nā fitnatal li-l-qaumi-ẓ-ẓālimīn. Wa najji-nā bi-raḥmati-ka mina-l-qaumi-l-kāfirīn.

رَبَّنَا لَا تَجْعَلْنَا فِتْنَةً لِّلْقَوْمِ الظّٰلِمِيْنَ ۙ
وَنَجِّنَا بِرَحْمَتِكَ مِنَ الْقَوْمِ الْكٰفِرِيْنَ

"Our Lord! make us not a trial for the unjust people. And deliver us by Thy mercy from the disbelieving people." (10:85, 86).

Fāṭira-s-samāwāti wa-l-ar<u>dz</u>i anta waliyyī fi-d dunyā wa-l-ā<u>kh</u>irati tawaffa-nī Musliman wa alḥiq-nī bi-ṣ-ṣāliḥīn.

فَاطِرَ السَّمٰوٰتِ وَالْأَرْضِ قف
أَنْتَ وَلِيّٖ فِي الدُّنْيَا وَالْآخِرَةِ ج
تَوَفَّنِيْ مُسْلِمًا وَّأَلْحِقْنِيْ بِالصّٰلِحِيْنَ

"Originator of the heavens and the earth, Thou art my Friend in this world and the Hereafter. Make me die in submission and join me with the righteous." (12:101).

Rabbi adkhil nī mudkhala ṣidqin wa akhrij-nī mukhraja ṣidqin wa-j'al-lī mil ladun-ka sulṭānan naṣīrā.

رب أدخلني مدخل صدق
وأخرجني مخرج صدق واجعل
لي من لدنك سلطانا نصيرا

"My Lord, make me enter a truthful entering, and make me go forth a truthful going forth, and grant me from Thy presence an authority to help (me)." (17:80).

Rabba-nā āti-nā-mil-ladun-ka raḥmatan wa hayyi' la-nā min amri-nā rashada.

ربنا آتنا من لدنك رحمة
وهيئ لنا من أمرنا رشدا

"Our Lord! grant us mercy from Thyself and provide for us a right course in our affair" (18:10).

Rabbi-shraḥ lī ṣadrī wa yassir lī amrī 'wa-ḥlul 'uqdatan mil lisānī yafqahū qaulī.

رب اشرح لي صدري ويسر لي
أمري واحلل عقدة من
لساني يفقهوا قولي

"My Lord! expand my breast for me: And ease my affair for me: And loose the knot from my tongue (that) they may understand my word" (20:25-28)

Annī massa-niya-dẓ-dẓurru wa anta Arḥamu-r-rāḥimīn.

أني مسني الضر وأنت أرحم
الراحمين

"Distress has afflicted me! and Thou art the most Merciful of those who show mercy." (21:83).

Lā ilāha illā anta subḥāna-ka innī kuntu mina-ẓ-ẓālimīn.

لا إله إلا أنت سبحانك
إني كنت من الظالمين

"There is no God but Thou, glory be to Thee! Surely I am of the sufferers of loss." (21:87).

Rabbi lā tadhar-nī fardan wa anta Khairu-l-wārithīn.

رَبِّ لَا تَذَرْنِيْ فَرْدًا وَّأَنْتَ
خَيْرُ الْوٰرِثِيْنَ

"My Lord, leave me not alone! and Thou art the Best of inheritors." (21:89).

Rabba-nā āmannā fa-ghfir-la-nā wa-rḥamnā wa anta Khairu-r-rāḥimīn.

رَبَّنَآ اٰمَنَّا فَاغْفِرْ لَنَا وَارْحَمْنَا
وَأَنْتَ خَيْرُ الرّٰحِمِيْنَ

"Our Lord, we believe, so forgive us and have mercy on us, and Thou are the Best of those who show mercy." (23:109).

Rabba-nā hab la-nā min azwāji-nā wa dhurriyyāti-nā qurrata' a'yunin wa j'al-nā li-l-muttaqīna imāmā.

رَبَّنَا هَبْ لَنَا مِنْ أَزْوَاجِنَا وَ
ذُرِّيّٰتِنَا قُرَّةَ أَعْيُنٍ وَّاجْعَلْنَا
لِلْمُتَّقِيْنَ إِمَامًا

"Our Lord, grant us in our wives and our offspring the joy of our eyes, and make us leaders for those who guard against evil." (25:74).

Rabbi auzi'-nī an ashkura ni'mata ka-llatī an'amta 'alayya wa 'alā wālidayya wa an a'mala ṣāliḥan tardzā-hu wa aṣliḥ lī fī dhur-riyyatī, innī tubtu ilai-ka wa innī mina-l-Muslimīn.

رَبِّ أَوْزِعْنِيْٓ أَنْ أَشْكُرَ نِعْمَتَكَ
الَّتِيْٓ أَنْعَمْتَ عَلَيَّ وَعَلٰى وَالِدَيَّ
وَأَنْ أَعْمَلَ صَالِحًا تَرْضٰهُ وَأَصْلِحْ
لِيْ فِيْ ذُرِّيَّتِيْ إِنِّيْ تُبْتُ إِلَيْكَ
وَإِنِّيْ مِنَ الْمُسْلِمِيْنَ

"My Lord, grant me that I may give thanks for Thy favour, which Thou hast bestowed on me and on my parents, and that I may do good which pleases Thee; and be good to me in respect of my offspring. Truly I turn to Thee, and truly I am of those who submit." (46:15).

Rabbi innī li-mā anzalta ilayya min khairin faqīr.

رَبِّ إِنِّي لِمَا أَنزَلْتَ إِلَيَّ
مِنْ خَيْرٍ فَقِيرٌ ۝

"My Lord! surely I stand in need of whatever good Thou mayest send to me" (28:24).

Rabba-nā wasi'ta kulla shai'in raḥmatan wa 'ilman fa-ghfir li-lladhīna tābū wa-ttaba'ū sabī-la-ka wa qi-him 'adhāba l-jaḥīm.

رَبَّنَا وَسِعْتَ كُلَّ شَيْءٍ رَّحْمَةً
وَعِلْمًا فَاغْفِرْ لِلَّذِينَ تَابُوا وَاتَّبَعُوا
سَبِيلَكَ وَقِهِمْ عَذَابَ الْجَحِيمِ

"Our Lord! Thou embracest all things in mercy and knowledge, so grant protection to those who turn (to Thee) and follow Thy way and save them from the chastisement of the hell" (40:7).

Rabba-nā wa adkhil-hum jannāti adni-ni-llatī wa'adta-hum wa man ṣalaḥa min ābā'i-him wa azwāji-him wa dhurrīyyāti-him inna-ka anta-l-'Azīzu-l-Ḥakīm.

رَبَّنَا وَأَدْخِلْهُمْ جَنَّاتِ عَدْنٍ
الَّتِي وَعَدتَّهُمْ وَمَن صَلَحَ مِنْ
آبَائِهِمْ وَأَزْوَاجِهِمْ وَذُرِّيَّاتِهِمْ
إِنَّكَ أَنتَ الْعَزِيزُ الْحَكِيمُ ۝

"Our Lord, make them enter the Gardens of perpetuity, which Thou hast promised them and such of their fathers and their wives and their offspring as are good. Surely Thou art the Mighty, the Wise:" (40:8).

Annī maghlūbun fa-ntaṣir.

أَنِّي مَغْلُوبٌ فَانتَصِرْ ۝

"I am overcome, so do Thou help." (54:10).

Rabba-nā-ghfir la-nā wa li-ikhwa-ni-na-lladhīna sabaqū-nā bi-l-īmāni wa lā taj'al fi qulūbi-nā ghillal li-lladhīna āmanū Rabba-nā inna-ka Ra'ūfur Raḥīm.

رَبَّنَا اغْفِرْ لَنَا وَلِإِخْوَانِنَا الَّذِينَ
سَبَقُونَا بِالْإِيمَانِ وَلَا تَجْعَلْ
فِي قُلُوبِنَا غِلًّا لِّلَّذِينَ آمَنُوا
رَبَّنَا إِنَّكَ رَءُوفٌ رَّحِيمٌ ۝

"Our Lord, forgive us and our brethren who had precedence of us in faith, and leave no spite in our hearts towards those who believe. Our Lord, surely Thou art Kind, Merciful." (59:10).

Rabba-nā 'alai-ka tawakkalnā wa ilai-ka'anabnā wa ilai-ka-l-maṣīr. Rabba-nā lā taj'al-nā fitnatal li-lladhīna kafarū faghfir la-nā Rabba-nā inna-ka anta-l-'Azīz-ul-Ḥakīm.

رَبَّنَا عَلَيْكَ تَوَكَّلْنَا وَإِلَيْكَ أَنَبْنَا
وَإِلَيْكَ الْمَصِيرُ ۝ رَبَّنَا لَا تَجْعَلْنَا
فِتْنَةً لِّلَّذِينَ كَفَرُوا وَاغْفِرْ لَنَا
رَبَّنَا إِنَّكَ أَنتَ الْعَزِيزُ الْحَكِيمُ

"Our Lord! on Thee do we rely, and to Thee do we turn, and to Thee is the eventual coming. Our Lord! do not make us a trial for those who disbelieve and forgive us, our Lord! surely thou art the Mighty, the Wise" (60:4, 5).

1. On going to bed:

Allāhu-mma aslamtu nafsī ilai-ka wa wajjahtu wajhī ilai-ka wa fawwadztu amrī ilai-ka wa aljā'tu ẓahrī ilai-ka raghbatan wa rahbatan ilai-ka lā malja'a wa lā manja'a min-ka illā ilai-ka āmantu bi-kitābi-ka-lladhī anẓalta wa Nabiyyi-ka-lladhi arsalta.

اَللّٰهُمَّ اَسْلَمْتُ نَفْسِيْ اِلَيْكَ وَ
وَجَّهْتُ وَجْهِيْ اِلَيْكَ وَفَوَّضْتُ اَمْرِيْ
اِلَيْكَ وَاَلْجَاْتُ ظَهْرِيْ اِلَيْكَ رَغْبَةً
وَّرَهْبَةً اِلَيْكَ لَا مَلْجَاَ وَلَا مَنْجَاَ
مِنْكَ اِلَّا اِلَيْكَ اٰمَنْتُ بِكِتَابِكَ الَّذِيْ
اَنْزَلْتَ وَنَبِيِّكَ الَّذِيْ اَرْسَلْتَ

"O Allāh! I give my soul into Thy charge and I turn my face to Thee and I entrust my affair into Thy hands and I seek refuge for my back in Thee, making my humble petition to Thee and fearing Thee; there is no refuge and no deliverance but in Thee; I believe in Thy Book which Thou hast revealed and Thy Prophet whom Thou hast sent."

2. On arising from sleep:

Al-ḥamdu li-llāhi-lladhī aḥyā-nā ba'da mā amāta-nā wa ilai-hi-n-nushūr. Lā ilāha illa-llāhu waḥda-hū lā sharīka la-hū, la-hu-l-mulku wa la-hu-l-ḥamdu wa-huwa 'alā kuli-shai'in Qadīr.

اَلْحَمْدُ لِلّٰهِ الَّذِيْ اَحْيَانَا بَعْدَ مَا
اَمَاتَنَا وَاِلَيْهِ النُّشُوْرُ ۝ لَا اِلٰهَ اِلَّا
اللّٰهُ وَحْدَهٗ لَا شَرِيْكَ لَهٗ لَهُ الْمُلْكُ
وَلَهُ الْحَمْدُ وَهُوَ عَلٰى كُلِّ شَيْءٍ قَدِيْرٌ

"All praise is due to Allāh Who raised us to life after He had caused us to die and to Him is the rising (after death). There is no god but Allāh; He is one, there is no associate with Him; His is the kingdom and for Him is praise, and He is Possessor of power over all things."

3. On going forth from the house:

Bi-smi-llāhi tawakkaltu ʻala-llāhi Allāhu-mma innā naʻūdhu bi-ka min an nazilla au nadzilla au naẓlima au nuẓlama au najhala au yujhala ʻalai-nā.

بِسْمِ اللّٰهِ تَوَكَّلْتُ عَلَى اللّٰهِ اَللّٰهُمَّ
إِنَّا نَعُوْذُ بِكَ مِنْ أَنْ نَزِلَّ أَوْ نَضِلَّ
أَوْ نَظْلِمَ أَوْ نُظْلَمَ أَوْ نَجْهَلَ أَوْ
يُجْهَلَ عَلَيْنَا

"In the name of Allāh, on Allāh do I rely. O Allāh! we seek Thy refuge lest we stumble or go astray or we do injustice to others or injustice is done to us or we behave ignorantly towards others or others behave ignorantly toward us."

4. On entering the house:

Allāhu-mma innī as'alu-ka khaira-l-maulaji wa khaira-l-makhraji; bi-smi-llāhi walajnā wa ʻala-llāhi Rabbi-nā tawakkalnā.

اَللّٰهُمَّ إِنِّيْ أَسْأَلُكَ خَيْرَ الْمَوْلَجِ وَ
خَيْرَ الْمَخْرَجِ بِسْمِ اللّٰهِ وَلَجْنَا وَ
عَلَى اللّٰهِ رَبِّنَا تَوَكَّلْنَا

"O Allāh! I beseech Thee that I may be made to enter a goodly entering and to go forth a goodly going forth; in the name of Allāh do we enter, and on Allāh, our Lord, do we rely."

5. Before meals or drink:

Bi-smi-llāhi wa ʻalā barakati-llāhi.

بِسْمِ اللّٰهِ وَعَلٰى بَرَكَةِ اللّٰهِ

"In the name of Allāh and with blessings from Allāh."

6. After meals:

Al-hamdu li-llāhi-lladhī huwa ashbaʻa-na wa arwā-nā wa anʻama ʻalai-nā wa afdzala.

اَلْحَمْدُ لِلّٰهِ الَّذِيْ هُوَ أَشْبَعَنَا وَأَرْوَانَا
وَأَنْعَمَ عَلَيْنَا وَأَفْضَلَ

"All praise is due to Allāh Who has fully satisfied our hunger and our thirst and Who has granted us His favours and given us abundantly."

Al-ḥamdu li-llāhi-lladhi aṭ'ama-nā wa saqā-nā wa ja'ala-nā min al Muslimīn.

اَلْحَمْدُ لِلّٰهِ الَّذِيْ اَطْعَمَنَا وَسَقَانَا
وَجَعَلَنَا مِنَ الْمُسْلِمِيْنَ

"All praise is due to Him Who gave us to eat and to drink and He has made us Muslims."

7. On going to the bathroom (closet):

Allāhu-mma innī a'ūdhu bi- ka mina-l-khubthi wa-l- khabā-'ithi.

اَللّٰهُمَّ اِنِّيْ اَعُوْذُ بِكَ مِنَ الْخُبْثِ
وَالْخَبَآئِثِ

"O Allāh! I seek Thy protection from what is impure and unclean (or, from unrighteous conduct and evil qualities)."

8. On coming out from the bathroom (closet):

Al-ḥamdu li- llāhi- lladhī adhhab 'anni-l-adhā wa 'āfā-nī.

اَلْحَمْدُ لِلّٰهِ الَّذِيْ اَذْهَبَ عَنِّي
الْاَذٰى وَعَافَانِيْ

"All praise is due to Allāh Who has removed impurity from me and granted me security."

9. On entering a city:

Allāhu-mma innā nas'alu-ka khaira hadhi-hi-l-qaryati wa khaira ahli-hā wa na'udhu bi-ka min sharri-hā wa sharri ahli-hā wa sharri mā fi-hā.
Allāhu-mma ḥabbib-nā ilā ahli-hā wa ḥabbib sāliḥī ahli-hā ilai-nā.

اَللّٰهُمَّ اِنَّا نَسْئَلُكَ خَيْرَ هٰذِهِ الْقَرْيَةِ
وَخَيْرَ اَهْلِهَا وَنَعُوْذُ بِكَ مِنْ شَرِّهَا
وَشَرِّ اَهْلِهَا وَشَرِّ مَا فِيْهَا
اَللّٰهُمَّ حَبِّبْنَا اِلٰى اَهْلِهَا وَحَبِّبْ
صَالِحِيْ اَهْلِهَا اِلَيْنَا

"O Allāh! we ask of Thee the good of this town and the good of its residents, and we seek refuge in Thee from its mischief and the mischief of its residents and the mischief of what is in it. O Allāh! make its residents love us and make us love the righteous from among its residents."

10. On visiting a sick man:

Adhhibi-l-ba'sa Rabba-n-nāsi wa shfi anta-sh-shāfī la shifā'a illā shifā'u-ka shifā'an lā yughādir u saqamā.

أَذْهِبِ الْبَاسَ رَبَّ النَّاسِ
وَاشْفِ أَنْتَ الشَّافِي لَا شِفَآءَ
إِلَّا شِفَاؤُكَ شِفَآءً لَّا يُغَادِرُ سَقَمًا

"Take away the sickness, O Lord, of all people! and restore to health. Thou art the Healer; there is no healing but the healing which Thou givest; grant recovery which leaves no ailment behind."

11. On visiting a graveyard:

As-salāmu 'alai-kum ahla-d-diyāri mina-l-mu'minīna wa-l Muslimīna wa innā inshā'a-llāhu bi-kum la-lāḥiqūn; nas'alu-llāha la-nā wa la-kumu-l-'āfiyata. As-salāmu-'alai-kum yā ahla-l-qubūri yaghfiru-llāhu la nā wa la-kum antum salafu-nā wa naḥnu bi-l-athari.

اَلسَّلَامُ عَلَيْكُمْ أَهْلَ الدِّيَارِ مِنَ
الْمُؤْمِنِيْنَ وَالْمُسْلِمِيْنَ وَإِنَّا إِنْ
شَآءَ اللّٰهُ بِكُمْ لَلَاحِقُوْنَ
نَسْئَلُ اللّٰهَ لَنَا وَلَكُمُ الْعَافِيَةَ
اَلسَّلَامُ عَلَيْكُمْ يَآ أَهْلَ الْقُبُوْرِ
يَغْفِرُ اللّٰهُ لَنَا وَلَكُمْ أَنْتُمْ سَلَفُنَا
وَنَحْنُ بِالْأَثَرِ

"Peace be on you! O dwellers of the abode from among the believers and the Muslims! and we will meet you, if it please Allāh. We pray to Allāh for security for ourselves and for you. Peace be on you, O dwellers of the graves! may Allāh grant you and us protection. You are those who have gone before us and we are following you."

12. Going out on a journey:

Allāhu-mma innā nas'alu-ka fī safari-nā hādha-l-birra wa-t-taqwā wa mina-l-'amali mā tardzā.

اَللّٰهُمَّ إِنَّا نَسْئَلُكَ فِيْ سَفَرِنَا هٰذَا
الْبِرَّ وَالتَّقْوٰى وَمِنَ الْعَمَلِ مَا
تَرْضٰى

"O Allāh! we ask of Thee during this our journey righteousness and faithfulness to duty and the doing of deeds which Thou art pleased with."

Allāhu-mma hawwin 'alai-nā safara-nā hā<u>dh</u>ā wa-ṭwi la-nā bu'da-hū.
Allāhu-mma anta-ṣ-ṣāḥibu fis safari wa-l-<u>kh</u>alīfatu fi-l-ahli.

اَللّٰهُمَّ هَوِّنْ عَلَيْنَا سَفَرَنَا هٰذَا
وَاطْوِلَنَا بُعْدَهٗ
اَللّٰهُمَّ اَنْتَ الصَّاحِبُ فِي السَّفَرِ
وَالْخَلِيْفَةُ فِي الْاَهْلِ

"O Allāh! make this our journey easy to us and contract its distance for us.

"O Allāh! Thou art the companion in the journey and the guardian of the family."

13. When riding or driving:

Subḥāna-lla<u>dh</u>ī sa<u>kh</u> <u>kh</u>ara la-nā hā<u>dh</u>ā wa mā kunnā la-hū muqrinīna wa innā ilā Rabbi-nā la-munqalibūn.

سُبْحَانَ الَّذِيْ سَخَّرَ لَنَا هٰذَا
وَمَا كُنَّا لَهٗ مُقْرِنِيْنَ وَاِنَّا اِلٰى
رَبِّنَا لَمُنْقَلِبُوْنَ

"Glory be to Him Who made this subservient to us and we were not able to do it; and surely to our Lord we must return."

14. On entering a boat:

Bi-smi-llāhi majri-hā wa mursā hā inna Rabbi la-<u>Gh</u>afūru-r-Raḥīm.

بِسْمِ اللّٰهِ مَجْرٖهَا وَمُرْسٰهَا
اِنَّ رَبِّيْ لَغَفُوْرٌ رَّحِيْمٌ

"In the name of Allāh be its sailing and its anchoring; surely my Lord is Forgiving, Merciful."

15. When one is in distress:

Allahu-mma-stur aurāti-na wa āmin rau'āti-nā.

اَللّٰهُمَّ اسْتُرْ عَوْرَاتِنَا وَاٰمِنْ
رَوْعَاتِنَا

"O Allāh! do Thou protect us in our shame and take away from us our fright."

Allāhu-mma raḥmata-ka arjū fa-lā takil-nī ilā nafsī ṭarfata 'ainin.

اَللّٰهُمَّ رَحْمَتَكَ اَرْجُوْا فَلَا تَكِلْنِيْ
اِلٰى نَفْسِيْ طَرْفَةَ عَيْنٍ

O Allāh! I do hope for Thy mercy, so do not leave me to myself for the twinkling of an eye."

Yā Ḥayyu yā Qayyūmu bi-raḥmati-ka astaghīthu.

يَا حَيُّ يَا قَيُّوْمُ بِرَحْمَتِكَ اَسْتَغِيْثُ

"O Thou Who art Ever-living and self-subsisting by whom all subsist, I do cry for Thy mercy."

16. Before a looking-glass:

Allāhu-mma kamā ḥassanta khalqi fa aḥsin khuluqī.

اَللّٰهُمَّ كَمَا حَسَّنْتَ خَلْقِيْ فَاَحْسِنْ
خُلُقِيْ

"O Allāh! as Thou hast made me well in appearance, so do Thou make me good in morals."

17. When the first fruit is tasted:

Allāhu-mma bārik la-nā fī thamari-nā, wa bārik la-nā fī madīnati-nā Allāhu-mma kama araita-nā awwala-hū fa ari-nā ākhira-hu.

اَللّٰهُمَّ بَارِكْ لَنَا فِيْ ثَمَرِنَا وَبَارِكْ
لَنَا فِيْ مَدِيْنَتِنَا اَللّٰهُمَّ كَمَا اَرَيْتَنَا
اَوَّلَهٗ فَاَرِنَا اٰخِرَهٗ

"O Allāh! bless us in regard to our fruits and bless us in regard to our town; O Allāh! as Thou hast made us taste the first of it, make us taste the last of it."

18. After bath or ablution:

Allāhu-mma-j'al-nī mina-t-tawwābīna wa-j'al nī mina-l-muta-ṭahhirīn.

اَللّٰهُمَّ اجْعَلْنِيْ مِنَ التَّوَّابِيْنَ
وَاجْعَلْنِيْ مِنَ الْمُتَطَهِّرِيْنَ

"O Allāh! make me of those who turn to Thee and make me of those who purify themselves."

19. When facing the enemy:

Allāhu-mma innā naj'alu-ka fī nuḥūri-him wa na'ū<u>dh</u>u bi-ka min <u>sh</u>urūri-him.

اَللّٰهُمَّ اِنَّا نَجْعَلُكَ فِيْ نُحُوْرِهِمْ وَ
نَعُوْذُبِكَ مِنْ شُرُوْرِهِمْ

"O Allāh! we beseech Thy help in opposing them and seek Thy refuge from their mischiefs."

Allāhu-mma bi-ka aḥūlu wa bi-ka aṣūlu wa bi-ka uqātilu.

اَللّٰهُمَّ بِكَ اَحُوْلُ وَبِكَ اَصُوْلُ
وَبِكَ اُقَاتِلُ

"O Allāh! with Thy help I go forth, and with Thy help I attack and with Thy help I fight."

20. *Isti<u>kh</u>āra* or prayer to be guided aright when undertaking an affair:

Allāhu-mma innī asta<u>kh</u>īru ka bi-'ilmi-ka wa astaqdiru-ka bi-qudrati-ka wa as'alu-ka min fa<u>dz</u>li-ka-l-'aẓim, fa inna-ka taqdiru wa lā aqdiru wa ta'lamu wa lā a'lamu wa anta 'Allāmu-l-<u>gh</u>uyūb. Allāhu-mma in kunta ta'lamu anna hā<u>dh</u>a-l-amra <u>kh</u>airul-lī fī dīnī wa ma'ā<u>sh</u>ī wa

اَللّٰهُمَّ اِنِّيْ اَسْتَخِيْرُكَ بِعِلْمِكَ وَ
اَسْتَقْدِرُكَ بِقُدْرَتِكَ وَاَسْاَلُكَ
مِنْ فَضْلِكَ الْعَظِيْمِ فَاِنَّكَ تَقْدِرُ
وَلَا اَقْدِرُ وَتَعْلَمُ وَلَا اَعْلَمُ وَاَنْتَ
عَلَّامُ الْغُيُوْبِ اَللّٰهُمَّ اِنْ كُنْتَ تَعْلَمُ
اَنَّ هٰذَا الْاَمْرَ خَيْرٌ لِّيْ فِيْ دِيْنِيْ
وَمَعَاشِيْ وَعَاقِبَةِ اَمْرِيْ فَاقْدِرْ

'āqibati amrī faq-dir-hu lī wa yassir-hu lī <u>th</u>umma bārik lī fi-hī wa in kunta ta'lamu anna hā<u>dh</u>a-l-amra <u>sh</u>arrul-lī fī dīnī wa ma'ā<u>sh</u>ī wa 'āqibati amrī fa-ṣrif-hu 'an-nī wa ṣrif-nī 'an-hu wa-qdur li-ya-l-<u>kh</u>aira ḥai<u>th</u>u kāna <u>th</u>umma ar<u>dz</u>i-nī bi-hī.

لِي وَيَسِّرْهُ لِي ثُمَّ بَارِكْ
لِي فِيهِ وَإِنْ كُنْتَ تَعْلَمُ أَنَّ
هٰذَا الْأَمْرَ شَرٌّ لِّي فِي دِينِي
وَمَعَاشِي وَعَاقِبَةِ أَمْرِي فَاصْرِفْهُ
عَنِّي وَاصْرِفْنِي عَنْهُ وَاقْدُرْ لِيَ
الْخَيْرَ حَيْثُ كَانَ ثُمَّ أَرْضِنِي بِهِ

"O Allāh! I beseech of Thee good by Thy knowledge and ask of Thee power out of Thy power and beg of Thee of Thy great grace, for Thou hast power and I have not the power, and Thou knowest and I do not know and Thou art the Great Knower of the secrets. O Allāh! if Thou knowest that this affair is good for me with respect to my faith and the means of my sustenance and in the end, grant me access to it and make it easy for me then bless me in it; and if Thou knowest that this affair is evil for me with respect to my faith and the means of my sustenance and in the end, then turn it away from me and turn me away from it, and make accessible to me good wherever it is, then grant me satisfaction in it."

Short Phrases Of Daily Use Which Every Muslim Ought To Know

1. *Bi-smi-llāh.* بِسْمِ اللّٰهِ

"In the name of Allāh"

Every affair is begun with these words. The object is to make a man realize that he should seek the help of God in all affairs. This is an abbreviated form of the fuller formula which runs thus:—

Bi-smi-llāhi-r-Raḥmān ir-Raḥīm. بِسْمِ اللّٰهِ الرَّحْمٰنِ الرَّحِيْمِ

"In the name of Allāh, the Beneficent, the Merciful."

These are the words with which the Holy Qur'ān opens.

2. *Al-ḥamdu li-llāh.* اَلْحَمْدُ لِلّٰهِ

"All praise is due to Allāh."

These words are generally uttered when any good comes to one, as a kind of thanksgiving to God. Even the sneezer is required to thank God in these words when he sneezes. It is with these words that the first chapter of the Holy Qur'ān opens.

3. *Allāhu Akbar.* اَللّٰهُ اَكْبَرُ

"Allāh is the greatest."

It is known as *takbīr,* and the words are uttered whenever a man has to give expression to his own insignificance or to the insignificance of all creation before Divine grandeur. These words also form a kind of war-cry of a Muslim as indicating that he is not overawed by the numbers of forces opposing him.

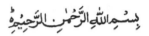

4. *Subḥāna-llāh.* سُبْحَانَ اللّٰهِ

"Glory to Allāh"

or

"Allāh is free from all imperfections."

These words are used when a man has to give expression to the fact that he is not free from imperfections or that he has made an error. They are used also when a man sees another making a mistake.

5. *Astaghfiru-llāh.* اَسْتَغْفِرُ اللّٰهَ

"I seek the protection of Allāh."

This is a prayer to which a man should resort very often, and the words are also used when one sees a thing which he should avoid. It is known as *istighfār* which means the seeking of Divine protection from the commission of sin as well as from the punishment of sin when it has been committed, and the more often a man resorts to it the farther away he is from the liability of falling into sin. The fuller form of *istighfār* is as follows:—

Astaghfiru-llāha Rabbī min kulli dhanbin wa 'atūbu ilai-hi.

اَسْتَغْفِرُ اللّٰهَ رَبِّيْ مِنْ كُلِّ
ذَنْبٍ وَّاَتُوْبُ اِلَيْهِ

"I seek the protection of Allāh from every fault and I do turn to Him."

6. *Lā haula wa lā quwwata illā bi-llāh.* لَا حَوْلَ وَلَا قُوَّةَ اِلَّا بِاللّٰهِ

"There is no strength nor power but in Allāh."

These words indicate that a man has not the strength to turn away from what is evil nor the power to adopt the course of good unless God gives him such strength or power, and they are used to give expression to reliance on God in all matters.

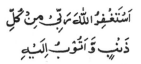

7. *In shā'a-llāh.* إِنْ شَآءَ اللّٰهُ

"If it please Allāh."

When a man undertakes to do a thing, he uses these words to indicate that though he is fully determined to do it, yet, maybe, it is ordained by God otherwise.

8. *Mā shā'a-llāh.* مَا شَآءَ اللّٰهُ

"It is as Allāh has pleased."

When one feels admiration for a person or a thing, he uses these words as showing that all good comes from God.

9. *Ḥasbiya-llāh.* حَسْبِيَ اللّٰهُ
Ḥasbu-na llāh. حَسْبُنَا اللّٰهُ

"May Allāh suffice me."

"May Allāh suffice us."

The words are used to show that it is God alone Who saves a man from stumbling and from all kinds of errors and afflictions.

10. *Innā li-llāhi wa innā ilai-hi rāji'ūn.* إِنَّا لِلّٰهِ وَإِنَّا إِلَيْهِ رَاجِعُوْنَ

"Surely we are Allāh's and to Him we shall return."

These words are used when one receives the news of the death of a person or of loss of any kind to himself or to another. The words indicate that loss of life or property to man is only part of a Divine scheme, and that he should not indulge too much in the pleasures of this life nor grieve too much when he meets with an adversity.

11. *As-salāmu 'alaikum.* اَلسَّلَامُ عَلَيْكُمْ
Wa 'alai-kumu-s-salām. وَعَلَيْكُمُ السَّلَامُ

"Peace be on you!"

"And on you be peace!"

The first form is that in which one Muslim greets his brother, and the second is that in which the greeting is returned. An enlarged form is as follows:—

As-salāmu 'alaikum wa raḥmatu-llāhi wa barakātuh. اَلسَّلَامُ عَلَيْكُمْ وَرَحْمَةُ اللّٰهِ وَبَرَكَاتُهٗ

Wa 'alai-kumu-s-salāmu wa raḥmatu-llāhi wa barakātuh. وَعَلَيْكُمُ السَّلَامُ وَرَحْمَةُ اللّٰهِ وَبَرَكَاتُهٗ

"Peace be on you and the mercy of Allāh and His blessings."

"And on you be peace, and the mercy of Allāh and His blessings."

12. *Jazā-ka-llāh.* جَزَاكَ اللّٰهُ

Jazā-ka-llāh u khairā. جَزَاكَ اللّٰهُ خَيْرًا

"May Allāh reward thee."

"May Allāh give you a goodly reward."

When a Muslim receives a gift from another or when he receives any good, he thanks the bestower of the gift or the doer of good in either of these forms.

13. *Bāraka-llāh.* بَارَكَ اللّٰهُ

"May Allāh bless (you)."

When a person sees any good in his brother, he addresses him in these words, meaning that good may be granted to him in a greater measure and that it may never be cut off.

14. *Ḥasbu-ka-llāh.* حَسْبُكَ اللّٰهُ

"May Allāh suffice thee."

In these words a Muslim addresses his brother Muslim when he sees him stumble or fall into error.

15. *Yarḥamu-ka-llāh.* يَرْحَمُكَ اللّٰهُ

"May Allāh have mercy on thee."

In these words a Muslim prays for his brother when he sees him in distress.

اياتها ٧ (١) سُورَةُ الْفَاتِحَةِ مَكِّيَّةٌ ركوعها ١

CHAPTER 1

Al-Fātiḥah: The Opening

(REVEALED AT MAKKAH: 7 *verses*)

The *Fātiḥah* or the *Opening* is known under various other names. It is spoken of as the *Seven Oft-repeated Verses* in the Qur'ān itself (15:87), because its seven verses are constantly repeated by every Muslim in his prayers. It is spoken of as the *Fātiḥat al-Kitāb* or the *Opening of the Book* in a saying of the Holy Prophet, in which it is said that "no prayer is complete without the recitation of *Fātiḥat al-Kitab*" (B. 10:95). Hence it is also called *Sūrat al-Ṣalāt*, i.e. the *chapter of Prayer*, being essential to every prayer whether performed in congregation or in private. It is also called *Sūrat al-Du'ā*, i.e., the *chapter of Supplication*, because the entire chapter is a supplication or a prayer to the Great Master. It is also known as *Umm al-Kitāb*, i.e., *the Basis of the Book*, because it contains the whole of the Qur'an as it were in a nutshell. Some of the other names given to this chapter are *the Praise, the Thanksgiving, the Foundation, the Treasure, the Whole, the Sufficient, the Healer* and *the Healing*.

Al-Fātiḥah contains seven verses in a single section, and was revealed at Makkah, being without doubt one of the earliest revelations. It is a fact that the *Fātiḥah* formed an essential part of the Muslim prayers from the earliest days when prayer was made obligatory, and there is a vast mass of evidence showing that this happened very early after the Prophet's Call. For not only is the fact referred to in the earliest revelations, such as the 73rd chapter, but there are also other historical incidents showing that prayer was observed by the earliest Muslim converts.

The chapter is headed by the words *Bi-smi-llāh al-Raḥmān al-Raḥīm*, which also head every one of the other 113 chapters of the Holy Qur'ān with the exception of one only, the ninth, while the same sentence occurs once in the middle of a chapter, viz., in 27:30, thus occurring 114 times in the Holy Qur'ān. The phrase has besides acquired such a wide usage among the Muslims that it is the first thing which a Muslim child learns, and in his everyday affairs the *Bismillāh* is the first word which a Muslim utters.

The *Bismillāh* is the quintessence of the chapter *Fātiḥah*, in the same manner as the latter is the quintessence of the Qur'ān itself. By commencing every important affair with the *Bismillāh*, the Muslim in fact shows in the midst of his everyday life affairs that the right attitude of the human mind towards the Great Mind of the universe is that it should always seek a support in the Mighty One Who is the Source of all strength; and Faith in God, thus, finds expression in the practical life of a Muslim in a manner unapproached anywhere else in the history of religion.

The *Fātiḥah* has a special importance as a prayer. Its oft-repeated seven verses constitute the prayer for guidance of every Muslim at least thirty-two times a day, and therefore it has a much greater importance for him than the Lord's prayer for a Christian. There is another difference, too. The latter is instructed to pray for the coming of the kingdom of God, whereas the Muslim is instructed to seek for his right place in that kingdom, which had already come, the hint no doubt being that the coming of the Prophet was really the advent of the kingdom of God about whose approach Jesus preached to his followers (Mark 1:15). The prayer contained in this chapter is the sublimest of all the prayers that exist in any religion, and occupies the first place among all the prayers contained in the Qur'ān itself. A chorus of praise has gone forth for it from the greatest detractors of the Holy Qur'ān. The entire chapter is composed of seven verses, the first three of which speak of the four chief Divine attributes, viz., providence, beneficence, mercy and requital, thus giving expression to the grandeur and praise of the Divine Being, and the last three lay open before the Great Maker the earnest desire of man's soul to walk in righteousness without stumbling on either side, while the middle one is expressive of man's entire dependence on Allāh. The attributes referred to are those which disclose Allāh's all-encompassing beneficence and care, and His unbounded love for all of His creatures, and the ideal to which the soul is made to aspire is the highest to which man can rise, the path of righteousness, the path of grace, and the path in which there is no stumbling. Thus, on the one hand, the narrow views that the Divine Being was the Lord of a particular nation are swept off before the mention of His equal providence and equal love for all mankind, nay for all the creatures that exist in all the worlds, and, on the other, the soul is made to aspire to the great spiritual eminence to which arose those to whom Allāh was gracious, the prophets, the truthful, the faithful and the righteous (4:69). One would in vain turn over the pages of sacred books to find anything approaching the grand and sublime ideas contained in this chapter of the Holy Qur'ān.

As I have said, the *Fātiḥah* is the quintessence of the whole of the Qur'ān. For the Qur'ān is a book which declares the glory of Allāh and teaches the right way to man, and both these themes find full expression in the *Fātiḥah* The fundamental principles of faith, the prime attributes of the Divine Being, which are the basis of all other attributes, the relation which ought to hold between man and his Creator, are all contained in their essence in the seven short sentences of which this wonderful chapter is made up. And to crown all, this chapter opens with the broadest possible conception of the Lordship of the Divine Being and the brotherhood of man, nay of the oneness of all creation, for the unity of the creation necessarily follows the unity of the Creator.

In[a] the name of Allāh,[b] the Beneficent, the Merciful.[c]

بِسْمِ اللّٰهِ الرَّحْمٰنِ الرَّحِيْمِ ○

1 Praise be to Allāh, the Lord[a] of the worlds,[b]

اَلْحَمْدُ لِلّٰهِ رَبِّ الْعٰلَمِيْنَ ﴿۱﴾

2 The Beneficent, the Merciful,

الرَّحْمٰنِ الرَّحِيْمِ ﴿۲﴾

3 Master[a] of the day of Requital.[b]

مٰلِكِ يَوْمِ الدِّيْنِ ﴿۳﴾

4 Thee do we serve and Thee do we beseech for help.[a]

اِيَّاكَ نَعْبُدُ وَاِيَّاكَ نَسْتَعِيْنُ ﴿۴﴾

5 Guide us on[a] the right path,

اِهْدِنَا الصِّرَاطَ الْمُسْتَقِيْمَ ﴿۵﴾

6 The path of those upon whom Thou hast bestowed favours,[a]

صِرَاطَ الَّذِيْنَ اَنْعَمْتَ عَلَيْهِمْ ۬ غَيْرِ

7 Not those upon whom wrath is brought down, nor those who go astray.[a]

الْمَغْضُوْبِ عَلَيْهِمْ وَلَا الضَّآلِّيْنَ ﴿۷﴾ ع

---

a. I retain the ordinary translation of the particle *bā*, but I must warn the reader that the sense of this particle is not the same in Arabic as the sense of the word *in* in the equivalent phrase *in the name of God*. *In*, in the latter case, signifies *on account of*, whereas the *bā* in Arabic signifies *by*, or *through*, or, to be more exact, *with the assistance of*. The phrase is in fact equivalent to: *I seek the assistance of Allāh, the Beneficent, the Merciful* (AH). Hence it is that a Muslim is required to begin every important affair with *Bismillāh*.

b. Allāh, according to the most correct of the opinions respecting it, is a proper name applied to *the Being Who exists necessarily by Himself, comprising all the attributes of perfection* (T-LL), the *al being inseparable from it, not derived* (Msb-LL). *Al-ilāh* is a different word, and *Allāh* is not a contraction of *al-ilāh*. The word *Allāh* is not applied to any being except the only true God, and comprises all the excellent names, and the Arabs never gave the name *Allāh* to any of their numerous idols. Hence, as being the proper name of the Divine Being and not having any equivalent in any other language, I have adopted the original word in this translation.

c. Raḥmān and *Raḥīm* are both derived from *raḥmat*, signifying *tenderness requiring the exercise of beneficence* (R), and thus comprising the ideas of *love* and *mercy*. *Al-Raḥmān* and *al-Raḥīm* are both active participle nouns of different measures denoting intensiveness of significance, the former being of the measure of *fa'lān* and indicating the greatest preponderance of the quality of mercy, and the latter being of the measure of *fa'īl* and being expressive of a constant repetition and manifestation of the attribute (AH). The Prophet is reported to have said: "*Al-Raḥmān* is the Beneficent God Whose love and mercy are manifested in the creation of this world, and *al-Raḥīm* is the Merciful God Whose love and mercy are manifested in the state that comes after" (AH), i.e. in the consequences of the deeds of men. Thus the former is expressive of the utmost degree of love and generosity, the latter of unbounded and constant favour and mercy. Lexicologists agree in holding that the former includes both the believer and the unbeliever for its objects, while the latter relates specially to the believer (LL). Hence I render *al-Raḥmān* as meaning the *Beneficent*, because the idea of doing good is predominant in it, though I must admit that the English language lacks an equivalent of *al-Raḥmān*.

1*a*. The Arabic word *Rabb* conveys not only the idea of *fostering, bringing-up*, or *nourishing* but also that of *regulating, completing* and *accomplishing* (T-LL), i.e., of the evolution of things from the crudest state to that of the highest perfection.

According to R, *Rabb* signifies *the fostering of a thing in such a manner as to make it attain one condition after another until it reaches its goal of completion.* Hence *Rabb* is the Author of all existence, Who has not only given to the whole creation its means of nourishment but has also beforehand ordained for each a sphere of capacity and within that sphere provided the means by which it continues to attain gradually to its goal of perfection. By the use of the word *Rabb* the Holy Qur'ān thus hints at the law of evolution which is working in the universe. There is no single word in English carrying the significance of the word *Rabb* — *Nourisher unto perfection* would be nearest; but the word *Lord* has generally been adopted for the sake of brevity. *Rabb* or *Nourisher to perfection*, however, includes both the physical and spiritual sides so far as man is concerned, His Word being the spiritual nourishment through which man is brought to perfection.

1*b*. The word translated as *worlds* is *'ālamīn*, which is plural of *'ālam* (from the root *'ilm, to know*), indicating literally *that by means of which one knows a thing*, and hence it signifies *world* or *creation*, because by it the Creator is known. In a restricted sense it is applied to *any class* or *division of created beings* or *of mankind* (LL). Hence *'ālamīn* has been translated as "nations" in 2:47 and elsewhere. The all-comprehensiveness of the Lordship of Allāh in the very first words of the Qur'ān is quite in consonance with the cosmopolitan nature of the religion of Islām, which requires an admission of the truth of the prophets of all nations.

3*a*. English translations have usually adopted *King* as the translation of the word *Mālik*, which is not correct. *Mālik* and *malik* are two different words from the same root, the former signifying *master* and the latter *king*. According to the rule of forming derivations in Arabic, an additional letter (as the *alif* in *Mālik*) gives the meaning a greater intensity (AH), and hence a master is more than a king. The adoption of the word *mālik* or *master* is to show that Allāh is not guilty of injustice if He forgives His servants, because He is not a mere king or a mere judge, but more properly a Master.

3*b*. The word *yaum* is applied in the Holy Qur'ān to any period of time, from a moment (55:29) to fifty thousand years (70:4), and may therefore indicate an indefinitely small or indefinitely large space of time. According to LL, *yaum is a time*, whether *day* or *night, time absolutely*, whether *night* or *not, little* or *not*; also *a day*, meaning the period from the rising of the sun to its setting. According to R, the word *yaum* indicates a *period of time, whatever period it may be*, and this is the proper signification. As there are ample indications in the Qur'ān that the Divine law of requital is working every moment, and there is nothing to support the idea that it will not come into force before a particular day, the law of requital referred to in this verse is therefore a law which is constantly at work, the day of Judgment being the day of complete manifestation of it. *Master of the day of Requital* in fact stands for *Master of the law of Requital*, as that law is working every moment.

The word *dīn* means both *requital* and *religion*, being derived from *dāna, he recompensed, judged, obeyed* (LL). In describing God as Master of the day of Requital, the Holy Qur'ān lays stress, on the one hand, on the fact that the Divine law of requital of deeds is working every moment, and thus makes man feel the responsibility of what he does, and gives prominence, on the other, to the quality of forgiveness in Divine nature so that the law of requital is not like a rigid law of nature but like the dealing of a Master Who is essentially merciful, as already described. In speaking of the law of *requital* after the two great attributes of *beneficence* and *mercy*, the aim is to show that requital is as essential a Divine attribute to bring humanity to perfection as the attributes of beneficence and mercy. Beneficence is exercised towards the whole of humanity, mercy towards those who accept the Truth, and through requital are brought to perfection those who do not accept the Truth. Their punishment sometimes takes the form of distress and affliction in this life but it will receive a final shape on the day of Judgment. Both the afflictions of this life and the hell of the Hereafter are really remedial measures to exterminate spiritual diseases, and awaken spiritual life in man.

It may be further noted that God may also be said to be the Master of the day of Religion, in the sense that spiritual awakening will gradually be brought about in the world, so that ultimately the majority of people will recognize the truth of religion.

The law of evolution is, in fact, working spiritually as it is working physically in this vast creation.

4*a*. The first three verses of this *sūrah* speak of the grandeur of God and the last three of the aspiration of man's soul to attain spiritual loftiness, while this, the middle verse, speaks of the relation of the spirit of man to the Divine Spirit. Here the way is pointed out through which man can attain to real greatness. It is through *'ibādat* of God which means *obedience* (*ṭā'at*) combined with complete humility (*khudū'*) (R), and through *isti'ānat*, or seeking help (*'aun*) from God. The idea of *'ibādat* (*service* or *worship*) in Islām is not a mere declaration of the glory of God, but the imbibing of Divine morals and receiving their impress through humble service to God; hence the prayer for Divine help.

5*a*. *Hidāyat* (guidance) means not only *showing the way* but also *leading one on the right way till one reaches the goal*. This is the significance here. Through Divine help man seeks to be guided in the right path until he reaches his goal of perfection. Man indeed stands in need of guidance and light from God in his everyday life affairs and is therefore taught to look for light in the right direction, for light from God. But he needs this light in a greater degree for attaining to the great spiritual goal. What that goal is, is stated in the next verse.

6*a*. Those upon whom favours are bestowed are according to I'Ab the four classes mentioned in 4:69, viz., the prophets, the truthful, the faithful and the righteous (AH) It is in the footsteps of these spiritual leaders of the world that the Muslim aspires to walk, the chief aim of his life thus being not only his own spiritual perfection but to try also, and lay down his very life, for the spiritual perfection of others. He thus also prays for the Divine favours which were vouchsafed to the righteous in the uprooting of evil and establishing good in the world. It further shows that according to the Holy Qur'ān the favours that were bestowed upon the prophets — the gift of Divine revelation being one of them — can still be bestowed upon the righteous who follow the right way. It should, however, be borne in mind that prophethood and revelation are two different things, because the gift of revelation was, according to the express teachings of the Holy Qur'ān, granted to others than prophets as well; as, for instance, to the mother of Moses (20:38) and to the disciples of Jesus Christ (5:111). This gift of revelation or being spoken to by God, according to most authentic hadith, will be granted to the righteous among the Holy Prophet's followers — *there will be among them men to whom God will speak though they would not be prophets* (B. 62:6).

7*a*. The Muslims are warned here that even after receiving Divine favours they may incur Divine displeasure and go astray from the path which leads to the goal of perfection, and this is what the prayer of v. 7 aims at. The Holy Qur'ān speaks of the Jews as incurring Divine displeasure (2:61, 90; 3:112; 5:60) and it speaks of the Christians as having gone astray (5:77), and the Prophet is reported to have said: "Those upon whom wrath is brought down are the Jews and those who went astray are the Christians" (Tr. 44:2). Of course, the words are only explanatory and do not limit the significance of the original words used. The Jews afford an example of a people failing in righteous deeds, in carrying out the spirit of the doctrine while retaining the doctrine, and the Christians an example of a people corrupting the doctrine itself, and both these are the pitfalls of a people to whom the right direction has been pointed out. Again, the Jews and the Christians afford an example of the two extremes, the Jews rejecting Jesus, a prophet of God, as a liar, and doing their utmost to slay him, and the Christians raising a mortal prophet to the dignity of Godhead. The Muslims are thus taught a prayer that they may neither fail in good deeds while retaining the letter of the law, nor corrupt the doctrine, and that they may be kept on the middle path, avoiding either extreme.